PRAYERS
FOR MY
TEEN

MARK GREGSTON

HARVEST HOUSE PUBLISHERS

EUGENE, OREGON

PRAYERS FOR MY TEEN
Copyright © 2010 by Mark Gregston
Published by Harvest House Publishers
Eugene, Oregon 97402
www.harvesthousepublishers.com

ISBN 978-0-7369-2844-1

Printed in the United States of America

10 11 12 13 14 15 16 17 18 / BP-SK / 10 9 8 7 6 5 4 3 2 1

To my granddaughters, Maile Elizabeth and Macie Blake. You both are truly gifts from the Lord, and I will always love, cherish, and pray for you.

Acknowledgments

A special thanks to Sam Sheeley for your help in all we do at Heartlight to meet the needs of parents across the country. Your friendship is priceless, and your love for teens immeasurable.

Special thanks also to Blake and Melissa Nelson, my son-in-law and daughter, who keep Heartlight running while I scurry around the country helping other families.

Thanks to all the Heartlight staff members for your dedication to our mission and your prayers for me.

Thank you to Roger Kemp (and K.T. and Jessica) for your friendship and dedication to the mission of helping parents and teens.

Thanks to Tim Kimmell and James MacDonald for your encouragement and friendship.

Thanks to Dave and Tammee Bolthouse for your willingness to help struggling teens and their families.

And last, but definitely not least, thanks to my wife, Jan, for your unwavering support and encouragement. I've made two great decision in my life: to accept Christ into my life and to ask you to marry me and spend your life with me.

Introduction

Parenting is rarely like a pleasant but slightly boring turn on a carousel. It's usually more like a heart-stopping and unpredictable roller-coaster ride. In both experiences, the destination is never in question. But the roller coaster has more ups, downs, and moments of terror. As soon as you think you have it all together as a parent and feel as if you've reached a high point, you're suddenly slammed into yet another dip, another turn, another uphill climb. One second you're right side up, and the next second you're hanging on for dear life and maybe even screaming at the top of your lungs. But oh, how much more exciting is the roller-coaster ride! And how much more challenging! How much more thrilling, even with (or perhaps because of) the butterflies in your stomach, the fear, and the uncertainty of what's around the next turn! On roller coasters, I've screamed out God's name like a little girl. I've done the same in the twists and turns of parenting.

Calling out His name affirms His presence, His power, and His purpose in my life. Regardless of how I pray—screaming from the roller coaster or in the quietness of my soul—I am reminded that just as there was a beginning, there will be an end. Prayer brings hope to my hopelessness and calms my anxiety when I need a reminder that I am not alone. Prayer reassures me that my confusion does not deter His plan. It calls me to look for the bigger picture, to embrace a larger view of whatever is happening, and to search deeper for meaning in the struggles and for purpose in the pleasures. Prayer reminds me that this parenting roller coaster is a ride like none other and that it draws on every attribute and ounce of strength I have to survive the ups and downs of the adolescent years and reach the end with relationships intact and training complete.

Prayer reminds me that the thrill of the parenting roller coaster is so worth the discomfort that I'm willing to crawl back into that seat and get locked in for another thrill. Prayer changes things—including me. It has a wondrous way of changing situations. It forces me to remain focused on what's important, and it helps me consider my teen from God's perspective. Prayer aligns my heart with His and connects my heart with His so that my plans for my teen fall in line with His.

Today's world sometimes seems to work against us. It's a tough time to be raising teens. In this confusing culture, all the parents I know need as much help as they can get. I hope this book helps you strengthen your connection with God during your teen's years.

As you use these prayers, you will notice that in most

of them, I've used singular personal pronouns for parents (*I* and *me*). I did that because you may be raising your kids alone. If you are married, fell free to insert *we* and *us*. Also, many of these prayers are written for sons and many for daughters, but I wrote them that way only to make them more personal. Every prayer can apply to your son or to your daughter.

After you read the Scripture at the top of a page, pause to reflect on it. These three questions might be helpful for you to consider: What is this passage about? What does it have to do with the title on that page? What are the most important words? Then, after you read the prayer that follows, stop again and ask, what situation in my home does this prayer address? Read it again and put a few of the most important phrases in your own words. Let these super-short prayers lead you to linger in God's presence as you bring Him praise, search your heart, and offer your requests.

I hope this book of prayers will help you enjoy the parenting roller coaster. When the ride is over, you'll realize it wasn't so bad, even if it was full of ups and downs, twists and turns, climbs and free falls, fear and relief. It wouldn't be fun any other way, would it?

Mark Gregston

Prayers for My Teen

The Need for Help

O LORD, hear my prayer,
listen to my cry for mercy;
in your faithfulness and righteousness
come to my relief.

PSALM 143:1

Lord, I need You...period. My teen unintentionally reminds me of that on a daily basis. I never knew that the challenges he faces every day would test all that I have taught him, said to him, and tried to demonstrate. Help me explain better, answer more wisely, listen more compassionately, and learn to laugh a little more. Help me be as faithful to him as You are to me. May I be a point of relief and refuge to my war-torn son. And may I offer hope in the struggle, as You do to me. O Lord, hear my prayer.

Joyful in the Midst

Be joyful in hope, patient in affliction,
faithful in prayer.

ROMANS 12:12

Heavenly Father, it's easy to be joyful, patient, and faithful when all is going well. But I've got to tell You, it's a little harder when things get tough—and they have! Life seemed so much easier when my child was young, and now that her adolescent years are here, I realize what I've been practicing for all these years. Help me to be more and more excited about the possibilities for her future even though I sometimes doubt or feel afraid. Renew my hope. Help me be patient in my affliction. And remind me with a gentle nudging throughout the day to come to You. May my hope in You bring me joy amid the struggle. In Your Son's name I pray this, for He accomplished all that I am asking. Amen.

Down and Yet Not Out

I recounted my ways and you answered me;
teach me your decrees.
Let me understand the teaching of your precepts;
then I will meditate on your wonders.
My soul is weary with sorrow;
strengthen me according to your word.
Keep me from deceitful ways;
be gracious to me through your law.

PSALM 119:26-29

Lord, bring to mind the things I have hidden away in my heart—the Scriptures I have memorized, taught, and displayed around my home. Remind me of all that I have learned from books and preachers and teachers. Help me never to forget the things You have brought me through, the many spiritual battles You have helped me to fight, and the endless displays of Your faithfulness to me.

And I pray that when my soul is weary with sorrow, You will use Your Word to strengthen and refresh me so I can finish the work You have given me to do.

Sustaining Faith

I have chosen the way of truth;
I have set my heart on your laws.
I hold fast to your statutes, O LORD;
do not let me be put to shame.
I run in the path of your commands,
for you have set my heart free.

PSALM 119:30-32

Heavenly Father, you are the Lord of truth, and You have taught me well. Help me to effectively impart that wisdom to my teen. Keep me from turning him off to the goodness of Your glory or the application of Your principles. Show me how to encourage him so he will embrace Your ways and not shun them. My prayer is that You will set his heart free as You have mine and that You will help him run in the path of Your commands.

I Need Your Counsel

I will instruct you and teach you in the way you should go;
I will counsel you and watch over you.

PSALM 32:8

Lord, I feel as if I'm all alone in the middle of a forest and I've lost my bearings. Things aren't turning out the way I hoped they would, and my teen is turning away from me—maybe even away from You. Sometimes I'm afraid that the way I'm parenting her just isn't working.

Find me, Lord! Show me the path, reset my compass, and give me assurance that we're headed the right direction. Lead me through the confusing landscape of my daughter's adolescence, and give me the strength to follow You wholeheartedly. I want so much to be the parent You want me to be—the parent she needs me to be. Thank You for hearing my prayer.

The Legacy of a Son

Sons are a heritage from the LORD,
children a reward from him.
Like arrows in the hands of a warrior
are sons born in one's youth.

PSALM 127:3-4

Lord, I know my child is a heritage and a reward. I am blessed because You are faithful and because You gave this gift to my spouse and me. Keep fresh in my mind the image of when we first brought our child home, and help me never to question Your thumbprint on his life. Help me to remain focused in times of trials, confident in challenges, and courageous in confrontation. Help me teach him as You have taught me. I ask these things all in the name of Your Child, Jesus. Amen.

Surround Me

Plans fail for lack of counsel,
but with many advisers they succeed.

PROVERBS 15:22

Gracious Father, help me find people who can walk alongside me, who can point out Your hand at work, and who can remind me of Your faithfulness. Lead me to those who can speak words of encouragement to me and support me as I walk this path.

And Lord, please surround my teen with people who will encourage her and not discourage her, people who will help her and not hinder her, as she and I wade through these turbulent waters of her teen years. Would You bring people to us who have walked this path before so we can benefit from the wisdom they gained on their journey? Thank You. Amen.

When He Won't Listen

Listen, my sons, to a father's instruction;
pay attention and gain understanding.

PROVERBS 4:1

Lord, my teen won't listen to me. He has turned a deaf ear to my words and is so caught up in his own world that he pays little attention to our family. Teach me some new ways to enter his world. Show me new opportunities to enter his life. Help me engage with him in new ways, see new things about his life, and build a bridge from his world to ours. And as You lead me into his world, help me give him the understanding and encouragement he needs to live successfully in his world and occasionally cross the bridge into ours. Thank You for hearing my prayer.

Help Me, Lord

O LORD my God, I called to you for help
and you healed me.

PSALM 30:2

Lord, I am thankful for the way You have used me in my teen's life. I am thankful for the way You have helped me through my own "stuff" so I can help her through hers. May my life be a testimony to Your many good works, Your healing of my hurts, and the careful attention You give to my heart. I called out to You, and You showed up! I hope to do the same for my teen. Make me like You, Lord; make me like You. Amen.

The Wise Tongue

Reckless words pierce like a sword,
but the tongue of the wise brings healing.

PROVERBS 12:18

Sometimes my tongue has brought healing to situations in our home, but sometimes my tongue has damaged my teen's life. Lord, help me control my tongue and be quick to listen, slow to speak, and slow to become angry. Bridle my tongue, calm my fears, and give me Your perspective in the heat of the moment. Lord, make me wise and help me love my teen and bring him healing, just as You have loved and healed me. I love You, Lord. Amen.

Brokenhearted and Wounded

He heals the brokenhearted
and bind up their wounds.

PSALM 147:3

Heavenly Father, my teen has endured some pretty difficult experiences and picked up some hurts that no child should have to carry. In the midst of her pain, she has lost her perspective of Your involvement in her life. I don't want my child to be wounded and brokenhearted. Would you heal her hurts and restore her to health so she may be whole again? My prayer is that she would not be controlled by the damage in her life, but by Your Spirit, who can sustain her through any situation. Thank You, Father. Amen.

Pleasant Words

Pleasant words are a honeycomb,
sweet to the soul and healing to the bones.

PROVERBS 16:24

Jesus, Your words bring refreshment to my soul and excitement to my heart. You say the right things at the right time. Your correction thrills me, and Your wisdom astonishes me. You are a breath of fresh air and an encouragement that brings a smile to my face. Please help me be with my teen the way You are with me. May You increase in my life as I decrease. Teach me Your deeper ways of loving those around me. Thank You. Amen.

A Father's Instruction

A wise son heeds his father's instruction,
but a mocker does not listen to rebuke.

PROVERBS 13:1

Lord, my son is one of the mockers who don't listen to rebuke. As hard as I try, I just cannot get through to him. Would You let me know that You're working with me on this? I feel so alone, so tired, and so worn out that I feel abandoned. I pray that You would cause things to happen in my son's life so he might turn back to You and away from the path he is on. I trust You in the good times, and I trust You in these not-so-fun times as well. Amen.

The Blameless Walk

LORD, who may dwell in your sanctuary?
Who may live on your holy hill?
He whose walk is blameless
and who does what is righteous.

PSALM 15:1-2

Lord, I want to be an example to my kids. I want them to know of my love, my faith, my commitment to them, and my dedication to walk with them during the best of times and the worst of times. Help me be the kind of person who pleases You and strengthens them. Empower me to keep my word, to stand for what I know to be true, and to never be shaken. And if things do get shaky, keep me focused and strong. May I provide my kids with a good example of how to treat our friends, neighbors, coworkers, and family. Help me cooperate as You make me more and more like You. Amen.

My Own Feelings of Shame

Therefore, there is now no condemnation
for those who are in Christ Jesus.

ROMANS 8:1

I've got to admit, Lord, that when my kids act out, when they embarrass me or don't behave the way I want them to, I take it out on myself and shame myself for their choices, behavior, and attitudes. Instead of allowing them to be responsible for their own actions, I feel as if their failures are all my fault, and I spend quite a bit of time beating myself up for their shortcomings, as if I am totally responsible for them. Help me to quit condemning myself for their poor choices and start loving them unselfishly as they become responsible. Help me know that their choices, good or bad, are not about me. I know I am accepted in You, but when these feelings of condemnation cloud my way, I get lost. Lead me on a path to health and wholesomeness. I ask this in Your Son's holy name. Amen.

Walking in Truth

Your love is ever before me,
and I walk continually in your truth.

PSALM 26:3

Lord, I want to always walk in truth. I want to proclaim Your truth with my words and reflect Your truth with my life. Help me to share the truth, the whole truth, and nothing but the truth. Help me assure my teens that I always love them and want to reflect the truth, and help them come to me when they are challenged by falsehood, lies, and deceitfulness. May the way I talk and the way I live agree, may they both be rooted in truth, and may they flow out of a heart that's filled with Your love. Thank You for hearing my prayer. Amen.

Speaking the Truth

I proclaim righteousness in the great assembly;
I do not seal my lips,
as you know, O LORD.
I do not hide your righteousness in my heart;
I speak of your faithfulness and salvation.
I do not conceal your love and your truth
from the great assembly.

PSALM 40:9-10

Heavenly Father, give me the boldness to speak up when I need to and to share what is on my heart without fear of rejection. I tend to sit back and not say anything when I really should offer my point of view. Make me Your mouthpiece; use me as an instrument in Your great symphony. Give me the courage to join in conversations because of what You have taught me. May I not remain silent when I see an opportunity to talk about Your goodness and faithfulness. Thank You for helping me, God. Amen.

When You Can't Keep Quiet

I will utter hidden things, things from of old...
what our fathers have told us.
We will not hide them from their children;
we will tell the next generation
the praiseworthy deeds of the LORD,
his power, and the wonders he has done.

PSALM 78:2-4

Father, sometimes I say too much, but often I say too little. Your mighty works in my life are just as important as what You have accomplished in the lives of others, so help me share my story with my children and grandchildren. I pray that the things I have heard, the things I have learned from walking with You, would bear fruit in my teens' lives so they may not have to stumble quite as much as I did. Amen.

Keeping Our Promises

It is better not to vow than to make a vow and not fulfill it.

ECCLESIASTES 5:5

Heavenly Father, I make so many promises to my kids that I just can't keep track of all of them. In the busyness of the moment, I forget what I have promised, so I don't keep my word. Help me to take my promises seriously, to make promises only when I know I can fulfill them, and to follow through on all that I have promised. May my teens learn that they can rely on my promises just as we can rely on Yours. And when I do fail, I pray for the humility and honesty to say I'm sorry and to let You change my heart. Amen.

The Joy of Grandchildren

Children's children are a crown to the aged,
and parents are the pride of their children.

PROVERBS 17:6

Heavenly Father, I hear that grandchildren are such a joy. And You say that I will one day be the pride of my children. Help me embrace that hope and realize that my investment in the lives of my children will eventually pay off. Someday my grandchildren will bring me joy, and my teens will be proud of what I have done for them. For now, I'll keep reminding myself of that and hold to the promise of what is to come. You have brightened my life today, Lord. Thank You! Amen.

When the Problems
Keep Getting Bigger

"Woe to the obstinate children,"
declares the LORD,
"to those who carry out plans that are not mine,
forming an alliance, but not by my Spirit,
heaping sin upon sin."

ISAIAH 30:1

Lord, as each day passes, things just seem to be getting worse. When one thing is fixed, something else breaks. When one promise is kept, another is broken. As a result, whenever I hear one shoe drop, I expect another to hit the floor any moment. Each day seems to bring a new challenge. Show me how I can turn Your plan into our plan in our home. I want so much for my teens (and me) to quit making things worse. Help us to stop "heaping sin upon sin" and to start living in the power of Your Spirit. I ask this with a heart of thankfulness, Lord. Amen.

Suffering and Glory

Now if we are children, then we are heirs—heirs of
God and co-heirs with Christ, if indeed we share in his
sufferings in order that we may also share in his glory.

ROMANS 8:17

Lord, I seem to be taking two steps forward and one
step back with my teen. We have good days, and then
we have bad days. Joy and then sorrow, more joy…and
more sorrow. I feel as if I'm on a seesaw of emotions as I
process the fun days and the not-so-fun days. The problem is that I let the suffering distract me from the glory.
I focus on that which is not going well rather than that
which is going very well. Help us to accept the good and
the bad, to learn from every experience and get the most
out of every season. Some days aren't exactly what I'd
hoped for, but I'm thankful You are always with us, and
You are good—all the time. I love You, Lord. Amen.

Who Is Exasperating Whom?

Fathers, do not exasperate your children;
instead, bring them up in the training
and instruction of the Lord.

EPHESIANS 6:4

Lord, I love my kids, and I know they love me. Yet sometimes they respond to my requests by arguing, quarreling, and challenging my authority. I ask a lot of them because I want so many good things for them. I can get a little picky about their lives, often reminding them and sometimes nagging them. Help me to know what to deal with now and what to save for later. Show me which issues are major and which ones are minor, what I should teach my kids and what they should learn from others. Slow me down and help me pick my battles wisely. I want to undergird them, not overwhelm them. Please help me, Lord. Amen.

Walking in the Light

I have no greater joy than to hear that my
children are walking in the truth.

3 JOHN 4

Lord, I look at my kids and wonder how in the world they are holding it together in today's culture. I would have been a mess given the same circumstances. Thank You for putting Your Spirit in them, for keeping them on Your path, and for helping them make good decisions and choices. And if they ever begin to stray from the things they've been taught, help me to gently lead them back to the truth. Thank You, Lord, for Your faithfulness to me and to my teens. Amen.

Lonely with Affliction

Turn to me and be gracious to me,
for I am lonely and afflicted.

PSALM 25:16

My prayer today, Father, is that You would surround my teen with friends that would meet her social needs. The world is tough and cruel at times, and a hedge of relationships around my child might help fend off hurt and bring affirmation. I pray that You would place good kids in my daughter's path and provide her with healthy opportunities for fellowship and encouragement. Today's culture doesn't always have her best interests in mind, so steer friends her way that will validate what she has been taught. Please keep my daughter from feeling alone and afflicted. I'm so thankful I can trust You to take care of her.

Always Teaching

Faithfully obey the commands I am giving you today—to love the LORD your God and to serve him with all your heart and with all your soul…Teach [these words of mine] to your children, talking about them when you sit at home and when you walk along the road, when you lie down and when you get up. Write them on the doorframes of your houses and on your gates, so that your days and the days of your children may be many.

DEUTERONOMY 11:13,19-21

Lord, use me to teach my teen how to navigate the tough and turbulent waters of his adolescent years. Help me use the experience You have given me and the biblical principles You have taught me to guide him through the situations he faces every day. Show me how to build our relationship so he is willing to learn from me, and make me aware of teachable moments—opportunities to share Your commands with him and apply them to his world. Thank You, Lord. Amen.

A Sure Foundation

When the foundations are being destroyed,
what can the righteous do?

PSALM 11:3

Gracious Father, my prayer is that You would keep the foundations of my child's life from being destroyed. May Your gentle and constant presence encourage her and remind her of the goodness and wisdom found in Your Word. I pray that she would recognize the importance of her faith, not only because she has been raised that way, but because she sees the need for a relationship with You. Keep her foundation secure, and may it always rest on You. Thank You, Lord.

My Teen Is Not My God

How great you are, O Sovereign LORD!
There is no one like you,
and there is no God but you.

2 SAMUEL 7:22

Lord, I love my kids so much that I sometimes make them the center of my world, and I know that's a burden they should not have to try to carry. Occasionally I find myself treating them like gods, almost worshipping all they do and revolving my life around their lives. I start thinking, feeling, and acting as if they *are* my life, and I am here to serve them alone. Help me to give my kids their rightful place in my heart and to give You Yours. Remind me that You alone are God, and You alone are worthy of worship. There is no one like You! Amen.

Boundaries

Like a city whose walls are broken down
is a man who lacks self-control.

PROVERBS 25:28

Father, I pray that You would intervene in my life and in my spouse's life. Strengthen us beyond what we have experienced before. Empower us to stand up for what is right, to set boundaries, and to get our home in order so we may provide a great place of training and preparation for our kids.

God, may our children thrive in the future. Guide them into all truth so they will turn to You, seek Your will for their lives, and become the people You intend them to be. May they never be like a city whose walls are broken down, but rather, may they be filled with love, joy, peace...and self-control. We pray in Your Son's name. Amen.

Adoption

Religion that God our Father accepts as pure and faultless
is this: to look after orphans and widows in their distress
and to keep oneself from being polluted by the world.

JAMES 1:27

Father, thank You for holding us in the palm of Your hand and comforting us during the tough times of life. I appreciate the fact that You reveal Yourself to us in so many special ways. Today I pray that You would particularly make Your presence known to any adoptive parents who are going through challenging times. Assure them that You know everything they're going through and that You will guide and strengthen them. Remind them that their struggles are normal, that their children will likely be fine, and that You have placed these kids in their lives for a reason. Father, give them endurance and patience so they will hang in there with their kids even when they struggle. Provide them with tokens of Your goodness and graciousness and those little rewards along the way to keep them motivated. Father, I love You and pray in Your Son's name for every child in this world who has been adopted. Amen.

Border Patrol

As the mountains surround Jerusalem,
so the Lord surrounds his people
both now and forevermore.

PSALM 125:2

Father, Your love for us is immeasurable, and You constantly protect and guide us. As Your presence surrounds us, help me to surround my family with helpful boundaries that protect each person in my home from outside attack. Show me how to set borders that define who we are and who we are not.

I ask for courage to do whatever is necessary to establish those boundaries and get our home in order. Empower me to be the parent my teen needs me to be. Strengthen me to do the things I can do and to trust You to do the things I can't. Lead me, guide me. Thank You for surrounding my family with Your presence. May I surround my family with borders that reflect Your great love for us. I pray in Your Son's name. Amen.

Giving Thanks

Let the peace of Christ rule in your hearts, since as
members of one body you were called to peace.
And be thankful. Let the word of Christ dwell in
you richly as you teach and admonish one another
with all wisdom, and as you sing psalms, hymns and
spiritual songs with gratitude in your hearts to God.

COLOSSIANS 3:15-16

Father, Your love for each person in my family is unending, and You are constantly at work in each of our lives. Even so, sometimes when my family is struggling, I forget to look for reasons to thank You. I pray that You would give me a sense of hope, an awareness of Your activity in our lives, and an assurance that You will continue to accomplish Your will in us and cause all things to work together for our ultimate good and Your glory. I know that You hear me as I pray, and I know that You will answer because You want the best for my family. And for those things, I can be thankful.

Open the eyes of my heart so I can look at our situation the way You see it. Father, thank You for using every situation in my life to mold me and make me into the person You want me to be. Yes, Lord, I am thankful for all those things. I pray in Your Son's name. Amen.

From Innocence to Adolescence

I came to you in weakness and fear,
and with much trembling.

I CORINTHIANS 2:3

Father, Your love for our family has remained constant through the years. You have stuck with us through thick and thin. As You have remained engaged with us, help me to remain engaged with my child as she grows through the difficult teen years.

I admit that I am often afraid when I think of my daughter being influenced by her friends and the media, being exposed to so many new things, and being tempted by a permissive society. Father, I need Your encouragement, I need Your wisdom, and I need strength to hang in there when the times get tough. Thank You for helping my daughter through this transition from innocence to adolescence, and thank You for helping me to be the parent she needs right now. I pray in Jesus' name. Amen.

Tell Me There's Hope

Anyone who is among the living has hope—
even a live dog is better off than a dead lion!

ECCLESIASTES 9:4

Lord, thank You for Your promises of hope. Evidently, only one thing is worse than feeling hopeless—being a dead lion! Your Word amuses and comforts me at the same time. I want to always believe I can have hope in any situation I face. But in all honesty, I feel like the disciple Thomas because I so often forget about Your faithfulness and sovereignty.

Right now, as I focus on You and Your Word, I know that You indeed know all, are all, and, I hope, will be all to me. But in the heat of battle, I often lose my focus, and my hope is gone. In those times, please remind me that You are there and that You care. Fill my mind with thoughts of Your goodness. Calm my heart with the assurance of Your great power and love. And when my teen is struggling and people all around me are losing hope, use me to point them back to You. Amen.

Knowledge and Understanding

The LORD gives wisdom, and from his mouth
come knowledge and understanding.

PROVERBS 2:6

Father, thank You for giving us everything we need, and especially for imparting to us Your knowledge and understanding. Help me to use those gifts to help my teen become more and more like You. When he feels empty, when he is confused, when he is angry or sad or lonely, give me the wisdom I need to gently guide him to You. Guard my mouth so I don't hurt him with my words. Calm my heart so I don't overreact when things go haywire. Fill my mind with the truth so I am not deceived by lies from the culture or from the forces of darkness.

Father, thanks for Your love. Thanks for always being with us, for never leaving or forsaking us, and for promising to guide us in every season of life—even adolescence. I love You and pray in Your Son's name. Amen.

Shifting Your Parenting Style

Who is like the wise man?
Who knows the explanation of things?
Wisdom brightens a man's face
and changes its hard appearance.

ECCLESIASTES 8:1

Father, Your love for me is absolutely amazing, and I need to remind myself of that because You have given me a tremendous responsibility as a parent. I'm in way over my head, but I know that You love my teen too and will provide her with everything she needs—including a wise and caring parent!

Lord, I tend to lose heart when I see my daughter make poor decisions and take a few steps down the wrong path. I pray that You would give me fresh wisdom so I don't get stuck in old ways of thinking and acting. Guide me toward new solutions as our family faces new challenges. Help me not be afraid to shift my parenting style when my daughter needs me to. I want her to see You in me and be drawn to You, especially in difficult times. In Your Son's name I pray. Amen.

Hope When Things
Spin out of Control

Sustain me according to your promise, and I will live;
do not let my hopes be dashed.

PSALM 119:116

Lord, my teen is spinning out of control, and I need Your help. I know Your love for me and for my teen never ends, but still, this is a tough situation. Lately I've felt as if I'm in the dark, so I pray that Your love and Your compassion would shine like a bright light and dispel our confusion. Let Your wisdom and understanding lead us from where we are to a better place.

Draw us to You and embrace us as we hold on to You for strength and perseverance. I ask for assurance that You will get us to the other side of this tumultuous time. Fill me with hope every day—even when our situation looks hopeless. Father, thank You so much for hearing my prayer, which I pray in Your Son's name. Amen.

Learning to Be Real

Similarly, encourage the young men to be self-controlled.
In everything set them an example by doing what is
good. In your teaching show integrity, seriousness and
soundness of speech that cannot be condemned.

TITUS 2:6-8

Father, when my teen is having a hard time, I pray
that every word I say to him would reflect Your heart.
Give me the right words to speak at the right time. Help
me control my tongue, bridle my thoughts, open my
ears, appreciate silence, and offer wisdom. May I be full
of integrity and sound speech and shine as a light in his
darkness.

And I pray that You would help me back up my words
by being a good example for my family. Help me to demonstrate a lifestyle of self-control, and help my son follow my example. Show me new ways to enter his life and
bring hope to what look like hopeless situations. Use me,
Lord, as an instrument of Your peace and a reflection
of Your love. May I be a mirror of Your image and help
those around me grasp a greater vision of You. Thanks
for Your example! Amen.

Embrace the Journey

For God knew his people in advance, and
he chose them to become like his Son.

ROMANS 8:29 NLT

Father, thank You for Your promise to always be with me. You are near even when I feel alone, even when I am in the wilderness, and even when my teen makes poor choices and takes different steps than I hoped she would. I pray for assurance that You are involved in our lives and in control of our situation, that You hold us in Your thoughts and have not forgotten us.

Sometimes I just wish this ordeal were over. If life had a fast-forward button, I'd be tempted to use it. But then You remind me to embrace the journey, to look for Your hand at work in every situation, and to learn the lessons You want me to learn along the way so I can become more like You. That's Your goal for me, so I want that to be my goal too. Thank You for working in my life. In Your Son's name I pray. Amen.

Remodeling Your Home

You see the trouble we are in: Jerusalem lies in ruins, and its gates have been burned with fire. Come, let us rebuild the wall of Jerusalem, and we will no longer be in disgrace.

NEHEMIAH 2:17

Father, You are the best kind of contractor: You can remodel my life and my home. I pray that You would strengthen my heart, renew my mind, and prepare me to face any difficult times that may be ahead for my teen. Transform our home into a haven of hope, a place of blessing, and a retreat from the pressures of life. May it be a refuge where relationships can flourish and each person is free to grow and change. Renovate my life and use me in my teen's life in a mighty, mighty way.

Father, thank You for skillfully building Your image in me and creating a beautiful environment for my family. I hope this construction job continues as long as I live! I am amazed that You care so much for me that You paid the full price for this remodel. I love You and thank You and pray in Your Son's name. Amen.

Connecting with My Teen

You were separate from Christ, excluded from citizenship
in Israel and foreigners to the covenants of the promise,
without hope and without God in the world. But
now in Christ Jesus you who once were far away have
been brought near through the blood of Christ.

EPHESIANS 2:12-13

Father, when mankind was without hope, You made a way for us to reconnect with You and with each other. Thank You! Now I pray that You would help me connect in some way with my teen so I may know his deepest hopes, his greatest concerns, and his worst fears. When he and I talk, help us not merely to exchange information but actually to connect at a heart level.

I pray that my teen would know me to be a gentle and respectful parent in the best of times and the worst of times. Help us to have fun as a family, to enjoy being together, and to find new ways of engaging with one another as we all grow older. Help each one of us to be sensitive and to intentionally pursue healthy relationships in our home. Father, thank You for my teen and for the opportunity to be involved in his life and to have him involved in mine. In Your Son's name I pray. Amen.

Reconciliation

Therefore, if you are offering your gift at the altar and there remember that your brother has something against you, leave your gift there in front of the altar. First go and be reconciled to your brother; then come and offer your gift.

MATTHEW 5:23-25

Father, I have plenty of experience at hurting people (sometimes intentionally) and being hurt. I have withheld love when I should have given it, and I have allowed anger, fear, and criticalness to control my feelings and thoughts. In these and countless other ways, I've allowed some things to damage relationships that were once important to me and have always been important to You. I'm sorry, and I ask for Your forgiveness and cleansing. I turn from these things...

...and I turn to You. Bring to my mind the name of a person You want me to reconnect with. Provide me with an opportunity to offer reconciliation to this person, and help us to heal our relationship. Lord, You have offered me grace, so now empower me to offer grace to those I have offended and those who have offended me. Thank You for leading the way and showing us how to be reconciled. As I draw closer to the people You bring my way, help us also to draw closer to You. Amen.

When They Won't Grow Up

Then we will no longer be infants, tossed back and
forth by the waves, and blown here and there
by every wind of teaching and by the cunning and
craftiness of men in their deceitful scheming. Instead,
speaking the truth in love, we will in all things grow
up into him who is the Head, that is, Christ.

EPHESIANS 4:14-15

Father, I know that one day my teen will get to the other side of her selfishness and unwise acts. I know that she will eventually grow up and that someday she won't be tossed around by the foolishness of this world. In time, she will learn to walk in a manner worthy of the calling she has received.

But how can I help her get from here to there? This in-between time concerns me. I know You are walking her through a process of becoming mature, so help me to cooperate with You. I don't want to do her more harm than good, and I don't want to enable her immaturity, so help me to give her reasonable amounts of responsibility. When she makes unwise and illogical decisions or stumbles and falls, show me how to help her get back on track. Bring to her mind and heart all that she has already learned, and I'll leave the rest to You. Thank You for helping me lead her through her adolescence. I would go nuts if not for You. Amen!

Rescuing Your Teen

A hot-tempered man must pay the penalty;
if you rescue him, you will have to do it again.

PROVERBS 19:19

Father, thank You for being involved in my situation. I need Your help—would You please give me extra courage and strength so I can walk through these difficult times with my teen? I ask for little reminders that even though the situation looks bad, You are involved in his life, and You will use every situation for his good. Give me wisdom and understanding so I can see possibilities for growth, even in seemingly impossible situations.

I pray that he and all his friends would continue to grow through all the struggles they are experiencing. Help them realize the importance of good behavior whenever they experience the consequences of bad behavior. God, this process is painful, but I know that shortcuts never help. Remind me to not rescue my teen from the results of his poor judgment, and keep me from accepting responsibility for any of his wrongdoing. I want to be a part of the process; not a part of the problem. Help me—and thank You. Amen.

The Prodigal Who Won't Leave Home

It is not fitting for a fool to live in luxury—
how much worse for a slave to rule over princes!

PROVERBS 19:10

Father, my teen is so comfortable at home, he doesn't want to leave! Sometimes he acts as if I should continue to treat him like a prince and make my world revolve around him. I wish he would move out, move on, and get a real life rather than hanging around and stealing mine.

But Lord, I do love him, and I want him to always know that I do. Help me to show him how much I care, even as I encourage him to take the next step toward independence. I confess that I'm often afraid that if I nudge him out of the nest, he'll fall—and I'll just have to clean up an even bigger mess. But I know that if he does, You will catch him and teach him to fly on his own. I ask for strength so I can set him an example of how to trust You and step out in faith. Give me boldness so I can express my feelings to him, and empower me so I have the fortitude to follow through and do what I know is best for him. Amen.

Training My Teen

Follow my example, as I follow the example of Christ.

I CORINTHIANS 11:1

Lord, sometimes I feel lost as a parent. What am I trying to accomplish? How am I to do it? Do I have what it takes? I pray that You would give me some clarity about those things so I can stay on target and be an effective parent.

Father, You have taught me so much, and I want to transfer some great principles into my teen's life so she will be a reflection of You. She's growing up in an extremely difficult and sometimes dangerous culture, so help me to provide a good example for her and to train her well—not to live in a zoo, but to survive in the jungle. Empower me to be intentional in my training, rational in my expectations, and consistent in their application. Please help her to be well-rounded, confident, and able to survive in the real world. I pray in Your Son's name. Amen.

Teens Gone Wild and Parents Gone Crazy

"For I know the plans I have for you," declares
the LORD, "plans to prosper you and not to harm
you, plans to give you hope and a future."

JEREMIAH 29:11

Father, I know that You don't intend for my teen to go wild, and you don't intend for me to go crazy. But honestly, sometimes I feel as if both of those things are actually happening, so I pray for Your comfort and for assurance that You are involved in our situation. Help me to keep a level head and not get so upset that I quit thinking rationally. And help my son to come back to what he knows is true.

Thank You, God, for having good plans for my son and for me. Thank You for giving us hope and guiding us into a great future. Empower me to be the parent my son needs me to be in this stressful time so he and I can enjoy every good thing You have in store for us. And until I see my hope fulfilled, help me to sense Your presence leading me in the right direction. I ask all of this in Your Son's name. Amen.

From Bad to Worse

Everyone who wants to live a godly life in Christ Jesus
will be persecuted, while evil men and impostors will
go from bad to worse, deceiving and being deceived.
But as for you, continue in what you have learned and
have become convinced of, because you know those
from whom you learned it, and how from infancy you
have known the holy Scriptures, which are able to make
you wise for salvation through faith in Christ Jesus.

2 TIMOTHY 3:12-15

Father, our teen has changed in the twinkling of an eye, and not for the better. She seemed to be one person one day and then somebody completely different the next. With her new friends, new attitude, and new demeanor, she's gone from bad to worse. She's rejecting what we've taught her and adopting a new mind-set that is contrary to what we believe. I try not to take it personally, and I know she's not really persecuting me, but that's what it feels like. Have I done something wrong?

Help me to continue in what I have learned and trust that the wisdom You have given me will bear good fruit. Father, please show me some creative ways to reach out to my teen and lead her away from the dangerous path she has chosen. I pray in Your Son's name. Amen.

Giving Grace

Because of the service by which you have proved
yourselves, men will praise God for the obedience that
accompanies your confession of the gospel of Christ,
and for your generosity in sharing with them and with
everyone else. And in their prayers for you their hearts
will go out to you, because of the surpassing grace God
has given you. Thanks be to God for his indescribable gift!

2 CORINTHIANS 9:13-15

Father, Your grace abounds in my life in so many ways.
I know I don't deserve the things You have given me.
You have blessed me beyond measure, and I am so thankful for Your provision.

Here's the hard part. I want to offer grace to my teen
just as You have offered grace to me, but he is disrespectful, disobedient, and dishonest. Offering him anything
seems next to impossible when he does stupid things and
makes me so mad. Yet I know that I have done the same
to You, and You never withdraw from our relationship. O
God, help me be more like You. Give me the courage and
strength to offer him something when he least deserves
it so he will understand the meaning of grace. Make me
like You, Lord; make me like You. Amen.

A Tough Sexual Culture

Flee from sexual immorality. All other sins a man commits are outside his body, but he who sins sexually sins against his own body. Do you not know that your body is a temple of the Holy Spirit, who is in you, whom you have received from God? You are not your own; you were bought at a price. Therefore honor God with your body.

1 CORINTHIANS 6:18-20

Father, sex seems to have permeated every aspect of our culture. My daughter wants to fit in with her friends, so she has fallen into a role she never really wanted to be in. I can hardly believe what I see and hear when she ignores the serious consequences of her sexual behavior. She is starting to stray, so I pray that You would go after her, touch her heart, protect her, and wrap Your arms around her. Remind her that she's not lost—You know everything about her and can lead her to where she really wants to be.

Father, I also pray for courage for everyone in our family. Help us to engage with her, to stand up and say, "You know this isn't right and there is a better way to go." Keep us from ever shaming her. Instead, show us how to walk with her and encourage her so she will learn how to please You in this sexual culture and make choices and decisions that will make her healthier and happier in the long run. I pray in Your Son's name. Amen.

Great Expectations

Quick! Bring the best robe and put it on him. Put
a ring on his finger and sandals on his feet. Bring
the fattened calf and kill it. Let's have a feast
and celebrate. For this son of mine was dead
and is alive again; he was lost and is found.

LUKE 15:22-24

Father, sometimes I fear the worst. I wonder if my teen
will ever make a turnaround. To be honest, from
where I stand, the future looks pretty bleak.

Yet I know that I always have hope in You. Just as the
prodigal's father watched and waited for his son to return,
I want to keep watch and believe that my son will eventually come to his senses and return to what he knows is
right. Chase away my fears, Lord, and help me to have
great expectations for our future together.

Father, show me how to "leave the light on" for our
teen, to assure him that he can make positive changes and
"come home" to the kind of life he knows is best. Whenever he thinks of me, may he know that I will always
love him and be available to help him get back on track.
And when he takes a step in the right direction, help me
to applaud his efforts, to welcome his cooperation, and
to celebrate! I ask all these things in Your name—with
great expectation. Amen!

Performance-Based Relationship

Let your conversation be always full of grace, seasoned
with salt, so that you may know how to answer everyone.

COLOSSIANS 4:6

Father, how thankful I am for Your love for me. It's
not based on what I do or how I perform, but rather
who I am. Our relationship is built on Your grace. I could
never thank You enough for that.

O God, please help me to cover my teen with grace too.
I want her to do well, but many times, my expectations
get out of hand, and I put way too much pressure on her
to perform. I tell myself I want what's best for her—for
her own sake, not because I need her to do well. Is that
really true? Search my heart, Lord, and show me if I am
basing our relationship on her performance. Help me to
assure her that I want our relationship to be built on love,
acceptance, forgiveness...grace. Help me communicate
that she can do nothing to make me love her more, and
she can do nothing to make me love her less—just as You
love me, Lord. Amen.

Understanding Your Teen's Inappropriate Behavior

Aware of their discussion, Jesus asked them: "Why are you talking about having no bread? Do you still not see or understand? Are your hearts hardened?"

MARK 8:17

Father, I get so confused when I try to understand why my teen does the things he does. I ache when I see him act the way he does, and sometimes I hurt so much that I can hardly see the real issues in his life. Oh, how I want to understand, to see, to know the truth.

Somehow, Lord, a hard heart evidently leads to blindness and confusion. Well then, soften my heart! I don't want to become so hard-hearted that I can't sense what's going on in my teen's heart. As I open my heart to You and to him, fill me with wisdom and discernment. Help me to perceive what's really going on in his life, and help me to see him from Your perspective. Help me be an instrument You can use to shape him into the person You created him to be—the person he really is.

Father, I love You and thank You for the way You work in our lives. Thank You for always being with us and standing beside us through these difficult times. I pray in Your Son's name. Amen.

Making a Plan

And this is my prayer: that your love may abound
more and more in knowledge and depth of insight,
so that you may be able to discern what is best and
may be pure and blameless until the day of Christ.

PHILIPPIANS 1:9-10

Father, I pray for Your wisdom, for Your guidance, for Your sensitivity, and for Your Spirit to fill me and show me what my teen really needs. I confess that sometimes I don't have a clue as to what is right for her, what is acceptable behavior, or what is the best path for her to take. This culture is confusing for my teen, and it's just as confusing for me.

Help me to be engaged, to be sensitive, and to be intentional about the way I lead her through her teen years. Guide me as I put together a plan of teaching, training, and releasing her. Help me to be purposeful and adaptable to my teen's changing needs so I will always be the person You have called me to be in her life. Let me know what I should take care of and what I should leave in Your hands. Fill me with hope and show me how this can work. Thank You for being such a wonderful parent for me. Help me to learn from You and be a great parent for my teen. I pray in Your Son's name. Amen.

Too Much Comfort

He longed to fill his stomach with the pods
that the pigs were eating, but no one gave him
anything. When he came to his senses...

LUKE 15:16-17

Father, You are so wise. Sometimes You allow me to do without some things, and even though I complain at the time, now I look back and realize that You were helping me to be more appreciative of all You have given me. Thank You for not always giving me everything I want.

I'm not quite as wise as You—my teen has never gone without. I have continually given him things, provided for him, and then offered him more. Instead of cultivating a spirit of gratitude, he has developed a huge sense of entitlement. I can hardly ever offer him anything anymore because he has become so demanding. He is so comfortable that he doesn't have any motivation to move forward in his life and start providing for himself. Father, help me quit giving him everything and feeding his sense of entitlement. Help me teach him how to work, be responsible, and provide for himself. I've worked so hard to make him happy that I've lost some of my joy along the way. Help me to say no, and perhaps when I quit giving him everything, he will come to his senses. Thanks, Father. Amen.

Helping Your Teen
Through Losses

You hear, O LORD, the desire of the afflicted;
you encourage them, and you listen to their cry,
defending the fatherless and the oppressed,
in order that man, who is of the
earth, may terrify no more.

PSALM 10:17-18

Father, where would I be without Your love? How could I have found meaning in the difficulties I've faced or maintained hope for the future? Thank You for always hearing my cry when I hurt.

Help me demonstrate to my teen that she can come to You under any circumstance. May she follow my example and draw close to You in difficult times. Assure her that You see her tears and hear her when she cries.

I also pray for my teen's friends. O God, make our home a place of rest, a place of welcome, and a place that is safe not only for my own children but for other teens as well. Fill us with Your Spirit so we will be sensitive and lovingly inquisitive. I want to be intentional and purposeful about this, Lord, so I ask You to teach me, lead me, and empower me. I ask these things so I can touch the hearts of those who are touching my teen. Thanks, Father, for listening and for acting. Amen.

Imperfect Parents,
Imperfect Teens

You are the light of the world. A city on a hill
cannot be hidden. Neither do people light a lamp
and put it under a bowl. Instead they put it on its
stand, and it gives light to everyone in the house.

MATTHEW 5:14-15

Father, even with all of our shortcomings, mistakes, and bad decisions, Your love for us never ends. No one else is like You, and no one loves the way You do except by the power of Your Spirit. And so...

Fill me daily with Your Spirit, and let the fruit of the Spirit grow in me—especially love. Strengthen my heart so I can love others, and especially my teen, with a love like Yours. Even with all my imperfections, may my love for him be so far beyond anything I could muster on my own that he recognizes Your presence in my life. Shine Your light through me so I can be like a city on a hill, a light on a stand, that points people to You. When I'm feeling disappointed or discouraged, remind me of Your presence so I will let You love my teen through me. My failures have never stopped You from loving me, so when he stumbles, give me the grace to be there for him and help him walk uprightly. I pray in Your Son's name. Amen.

Keeping My Belief
System Current

In his heart a man plans his course, but
the LORD determines his steps.

PROVERBS 16:9

Father, Your Word tells us that without plans, good intentions fail. And I've learned that outdated plans are usually not effective when my teen and I face current issues. I pray that You would show me the old-fashioned and ineffective ways that I do things so I can put them aside and move on to more helpful strategies. Bring new dreams and ideas to my heart and mind so I can see where my family needs to go. Give me courage, I pray, to stand firm in what I believe needs to happen in my family, and soften my teen's heart so she can hear and receive the things I have to say. Help her to see I'm trying.

I trust You to guide me as I look to You and make my parenting plans. But I know I'll never be able to construct an absolutely perfect plan, so help me be sensitive to You as You determine my steps. You've led me this far, and I know You'll continue. My best plan is to follow You! Amen!

Establishing Rules in Our Home

Make plans by seeking advice;
if you wage war, obtain guidance.

PROVERBS 20:18

Father, You love us in so many ways! You provide for us, lead us, strengthen us, make us more like You... and You give us some boundaries as well as some consequences for stepping outside those boundaries. Thank You for showing us what is right and for leading us on a good path toward a bright future. Your ways show us how to remain healthy and good and honorable and pure.

Father, just as You have shown me the right way to live, I pray that You will help me to establish a belief system in our home that will guide my teen through these challenging years. Help me to establish rules and consequences that are just and fair and that help us focus on the issues that are truly important. May the policies we agree on lead to better relationships with each other and with You. I ask for wisdom so the restrictions I set will empower us to live freely. Let our rules serve us well, and save us from ever serving the rules. Strengthen me to be consistent but not inflexible, encouraging but not enabling, engaged but not overshadowing. Thank You so much for Your guidance in this important task. I pray in Your Son's name. Amen.

The Schoolyard Jungle

Consider it pure joy, my brothers, whenever you
face trials of many kinds, because you know that
the testing of your faith develops perseverance.

JAMES 1:2-3

Heavenly Father, as I send my teen off to school every day, help me release him into Your care. I know that responsible adults are watching over him, but I also pray that You would protect him, guide and direct his thoughts, and keep him focused. Help him to sense Your presence with him all the time, especially when he faces important choices and difficult tests and trials. May the values and the principles and the teachings that I have poured into his life come to his mind and guide his thinking in each situation he encounters and each decision he makes.

O God, I don't enjoy tests and trials, and I don't enjoy watching my teen struggling through them either, but I know that You are developing perseverance in our lives. Eventually, we will look back and see Your hand at work in these confusing times. Help us to make the most of them. I pray in Your Son's name. Amen.

Will the World Hate My Teen?

If you belonged to the world, it would love you as its own.
As it is, you do not belong to the world, but I have chosen
you out of the world. That is why the world hates you.

JOHN 15:19

Father, when I teach and train my teen to survive in the world, I set her apart from some of her peers. I hold her to a different set of standards than most of her friends follow, and I desire for her to live a biblically principled life. I'm concerned that this will cause conflict between her and her friends.

She naturally wants to be accepted and to have a lot of friends. Would You remind her of Your presence whenever these two desires—to walk with You and to be accepted by her peers—collide? Touch her heart and draw her close so her relationship with You will help her make good decisions about her relationships with others. Bring Christian friends to her who will understand her, encourage her, and empower her to walk with You. And help her to be a positive influence on her non-Christian friends. May she stand for what is right, true, and honorable, and may other kids respect her for that and be drawn to You. And finally, Lord, I ask for assurance that You are protecting her, embracing her, and working in her life and in all her relationships. Thank You, Lord! Amen.

Married with Teens

Better a meal of vegetables where there is love
than a fattened calf with hatred.

PROVERBS 15:17

Father, I pray for my marriage today. Help my spouse and me to pay attention to each other, to care for each other, and never to let our love and concern for our teenager keep us from building a strong, intimate marriage. Protect us and turn our hearts toward each other so our child's struggles never come between us. Give us creativity and wisdom so we can agree on helpful strategies for guiding our teenager. When our teen causes turmoil, help my spouse and me to address it appropriately and with one mind so that even stressful times draw us together instead of tearing us apart.

O God, I pray that every time we look at our wedding rings, You will remind us of our vows to each other and the safety we can enjoy in our loving, committed relationship. When one of us is tired, discouraged, or frustrated, give us special grace so we can support and encourage each other. And help us to always have hope and remember that the struggles won't last forever. In Your Son's name I pray. Amen.

Mothering or Smothering?

For this reason a man will leave his father and mother and
be united to his wife, and they will become one flesh.

GENESIS 2:24

ather, I have entrusted my life to You, and You have
always been 100 percent faithful to lead me, protect
me, and provide for me. Now I pray that You would
help me entrust my teenager's life to You as well. I know
You will watch over and protect him, that You will never
leave him or forsake him, and that You will hold him in
the palm of Your hand and wrap Your arms around him
when he needs You to. Lead and guide him so he will
become the person You created him to be.

Lord, help me prepare our son for the day he will
leave home and be on his own. Show me how I can give
him more exposure and more responsibility in a way that
will help him to become more independent, trustworthy,
and reliable. I ask for wisdom and understanding so I
will know when to push, when to pull, when to back off,
when to engage.

In Your Son's name I pray. Amen.

Teens and the Internet

You have heard that it was said, "Do not commit adultery."
But I tell you that anyone who looks at a woman lustfully
has already committed adultery with her in his heart.

MATTHEW 5:27-28

Father, the world is speeding up, and I feel as if I'm
slowing down. Technology is coming into our home
so fast, I can't keep up. The Internet exposes my teen to
things I would never have seen at her age. It's even expos-
ing me to more than I want to see or read!

Father, would You give me discernment about all this?
Help me control these new influences in our home, use
them constructively, and block the intrusive and unhelp-
ful messages. I pray for Your guidance and direction, Your
wisdom and understanding, and Your boldness so I can
make appropriate changes in our home before the Internet
changes us. And if curiosity gets the best of my daughter and she falls into one of those Internet black holes,
help me to approach the situation correctly, effectively,
and appropriately. Show us how she can navigate wisely
through the Internet, take advantage of its strengths, and
avoid its dangers. Protect her when I can't, Father. I need
Your help on this. Amen.

Good Parents, Bad Results

How can you say to your brother, "Let me take the speck out of your eye," when all the time there is a plank in your own eye? You hypocrite, first take the plank out of your own eye, and then you will see clearly to remove the speck from your brother's eye.

MATTHEW 7:4-5

Lord, I've worked hard to be a good parent. I've loved my teenager, provided for him, taught him Your Word, and encouraged him in every way I could think of. But for some reason, he just hasn't responded well to my training as he has entered his teen years, and my efforts appear to be fruitless. I get disappointed and downright angry at times because I'm not seeing what I had hoped to see in his life.

Help me stop being so critical of him, start trusting in You more, and always look at the log in my own eye so I can see better ways to approach him, engage with him, and love him when he's doing things I don't approve of. I'm running a little thin right now and need some encouragement. Please, Lord, bring me some assurance that I'll eventually see some fruit from all my efforts. Thanks for all You've done already and will do in the future. Amen.

Implementing Change, Avoiding Chaos

Be strong and courageous. Do not be terrified;
do not be discouraged, for the LORD your
God will be with you wherever you go.

JOSHUA 1:9

Father, I want to be strong and courageous, but frankly, change scares me to death. My teenager is changing, and the culture around us is changing. But I'm not sure I'm willing and able to make the necessary adjustments in our home. I thought I was on top of things, but recently, the old ways of doing things aren't working so well.

Normally, I would rather run away from conflict than possibly cause conflict by introducing new rules, new boundaries, and new goals. I expect my teenager doesn't like conflict any more than I do. But if conflict is a precursor to change, and if change needs to happen before our family disintegrates, then I'll pay the price. Help me to know what changes need to be made and to implement them wisely. Changing course is scary for me, and conflict is even worse, but if we don't make some adjustments, we will surely experience chaos, and that would be worst of all.

God, I know I need to do this, and I want to follow through. Please guide me each step of the way. Amen.

Invisible Problems

This is the verdict: Light has come into the world, but
men loved darkness instead of light because their
deeds were evil. Everyone who does evil hates the
light, and will not come into the light for fear that his
deeds will be exposed. But whoever lives by the truth
comes into the light, so that it may be seen plainly
that what he has done has been done through God.

JOHN 3:19-21

Lord, I want to be the kind of parent whom teens feel
safe coming to when they have problems. I don't
want my own teen to hide things from me. So would You
make me an approachable parent? Someone who doesn't
judge, blow things out of proportion, rant and rave, or
shame my teenager? When she shares her burdens with
me, help me to not overreact but to respond gently, lovingly, and with truth and wisdom.

Then, Lord, after You've helped me to keep my cool,
would You also give me wisdom so I can handle the situation the way You would have me to? Show me how I can
strengthen and deepen my relationship with my daughter and still allow the consequences of her actions to do
their work in her life. And if she is secretive and deceitful,
Lord, open my eyes so I can see through the facade and
into her heart and mind. Amen.

Swimming with Sharks

Do not be misled:
"Bad company corrupts good character."

I CORINTHIANS 15:33

Father, help me never forget that You graciously sent Your perfect and holy Son to live in a very imperfect and unholy world so we could know You. And now You send us into the same world for the same reason.

I pray that You would use my teen as a positive influence, an inspiration, and a guiding light in his friends' lives. May they respect him and see him as a positive role model. Give him a sensitive heart that is open and inviting when he meets kids who are struggling. When he faces difficult decisions and tempting opportunities, bring the values that we have taught him to his heart and mind. Help him not to lower his standards or compromise his character for the sake of popularity. May he gain wisdom in each challenge and confrontation he encounters, and may he always have courage to stand up for who he is. Make him a "fisher of men," and protect him from sharks. It's in Your Son's name I pray. Amen.

Confidence in God

Blessed is the man who trusts in the LORD,
whose confidence is in him.
He will be like a tree planted by the water
that sends out its roots by the stream.
It does not fear when heat comes;
its leaves are always green.
It has no worries in a year of drought
and never fails to bear fruit.

JEREMIAH 17:7-8

Heavenly Father, I've worked hard to prepare my teen to live well when she's on her own. I've tried to love her intensely, discipline her consistently, and train her in the way she should go. As she makes more and more decisions for her own life, I ask that You would help her to trust You and to have confidence in everything she's learned. O God, may she flourish and bear fruit in good times and even in times of heat and drought. Build her confidence in You, and pour Your love into her heart so she is free from fear and worry. Thank You so much for watching over her. Amen.

The Underachiever

We urge you, brothers, warn those who are
idle, encourage the timid, help the weak, be
patient with everyone. Make sure that nobody
pays back wrong for wrong, but always try to
be kind to each other and to everyone else.

I THESSALONIANS 5:14-15

Lord, I'm not sure how to help my teen. He often retreats from the pressures of life and gives up. He acts as if he's retired or on vacation. I ache for him because he's not living up to his potential but rather settling for second best. I get angry when I see how unmotivated and lazy he is. He's unwilling to try to achieve anything, and he expects me to give him everything he wants. I'm not surprised that some people are idle, timid, and weak; I just never thought my son would be like that.

Lord, I look to You for wisdom. I open my heart to You and ask You to teach me how to encourage him. Fill me with Your Spirit so I will be patient and kind. Help me love him in a new way—with confidence in You and hope that a new approach may yield a different result. And Lord, thank You for treating me the way I want to treat my son. You warn me, You encourage me, and You are patient with me. Help me be more like You, especially in the way I help my son. Amen.

Teens Drinking

Stop judging by mere appearances,
and make a right judgment.

JOHN 7:24

Father, You saw my daughter come home drunk last night. I have feared for quite some time that she's been drinking, but I was afraid to address the problem. I never thought we would have to face this, but now I don't have a choice.

O God, I need to talk to her, but I don't want to get carried away because of my emotions. Show me how to engage in a helpful conversation with her and not allow my disappointment to control my response. Help me to discern the reason for the drinking. Was it a loss in her life? Has something happened that I don't know about? Is she self-medicating her depression? Is she just trying to fit in? Is she trying to escape from something? Or does she just like the way alcohol makes her feel? Help me see through her behavior to her motivation for drinking so I can offer a right judgment, consequence, and course of action to remedy the problem. And if my daughter and I don't have the resources to handle this on our own, please lead us to people who can encourage us and help us get to the root of the problem. Amen.

Getting Direction and Making a Plan

For lack of guidance a nation falls,
but many advisers make victory sure.

PROVERBS 11:14

Father, I don't know what to do! Everything I say is wrong, everything I do doesn't work, and my teen acts as if he despises my bodily presence. I am spent. I need someone to come alongside me, to offer some encouragement, to give me some direction…maybe even just to understand. Please lead me to someone—a neighbor, a friend at church, my pastor, a relative, or some other confidant. Help me find someone who can give me sound advice, someone who has been where I am and who has a plan. Lead me to the right book, radio program, event… anything that You can use to speak to me.

Lord, I admit that the things I've been doing aren't working. I'm willing to change, to quit claiming to be right all the time, to start listening more carefully to my spouse and considering other options. Fill us with Your Spirit so we can quit trying to convince one another that each of us is right and start working together as a team. Help us find middle ground and agree on a plan for the operation of our home. I trust You to help all of us enjoy being together as a family again. Amen.

When Your Teen Becomes Sexually Active

It is God's will that you should be sanctified: that
you should avoid sexual immorality; that each
of you should learn to control his own body in a
way that is holy and honorable, not in passionate
lust like the heathen, who do not know God.

I THESSALONIANS 4:3-5

Lord, we had hoped this wouldn't happen, but it has. Our teen has become sexually active, and I fear for the implications. She seems to be controlled by her sexual desires and not too concerned about taking Your Word or our family's values very seriously. Her friends and the media are so permissive about sex, she feels as if I'm making a mountain out of a molehill. But I know what Your Word says, and I want what's best for her.

Father, please help my daughter and me to have a helpful, respectful conversation about this. Show me how to connect with my teen and communicate the need for restraint in relationships. I've never had these conversations before, Lord…and I'm scared to death. Calm my heart, help me overcome my fear, and give me the courage to talk as if I could actually see You in the room with us. Thank You for always being near. Amen.

A Confusing Culture

God gave Solomon wisdom and very great
insight, and a breadth of understanding as
measureless as the sand on the seashore.

1 KINGS 4:29

God, just as You answered Solomon's request, would You give me deeper and broader wisdom, insight, and understanding about my teen? Open my eyes to his world and help me not to be so focused on my own. When I see things in the youth culture that startle or confuse me, fill me with peace and confidence in You, and keep me from overreacting or pushing my son away by saying something stupid. Teach me, Lord, so I can discern the influences and pressures he is facing, and help me know what is really dangerous and what is simply different from what I'm used to.

God, help me remember that growing up today can't be easy. Give me a heart of compassion and empathy, and show me how I can help my son through a difficult time. Bring to my mind some creative ways to move toward him and assure him that I am there for him. When he is weary and heavy laden, may I be a safe place for him to rest and be refreshed. I pray in Your Son's name. Amen.

Talking with My Teen

Jesus sent him away, saying, "Return home and tell how much God has done for You." So the man went away and told all over town how much Jesus had done for him.

LUKE 8:38-39

Father, I pray that You would open the door for good conversations between me and my teen. Help me to say something when I need to, to keep my mouth shut when I should, and to always be a good listener. Show me how to engage her and draw her out when she's tempted to retreat into her cave.

Lord, give me words of wisdom to encourage and guide her when she desperately needs me. Speak through me and remind her of Your restoring love and practical wisdom. May the words I use connect with her and be practical and applicable to her situation. Thank You for always communicating with us—fill me with Your Spirit so I can follow Your example. I pray in Your Son's name. Amen.

Kids as Victims

But you, O God, do see trouble and grief;
you consider it to take it in hand.
The victim commits himself to you;
you are the helper of the fatherless.

PSALM 10:14

Lord, I am so thankful that You care about people who are in trouble, people who have experienced loss, people who have suffered because of others' bad choices. When no one else seems to care or even notice, You do. What a gracious God You are!

Father, You know all the hurt my teen has experienced and his feelings of being abandoned. When he asks me why You allowed him to be hurt, I don't know what to say. I know You want better things for him—no teen should have to go through the things he has. Please assure him that You are there for him in the midst of his pain. Help me guide his hurting heart to You, and give him confidence that when he draws near to You, You will draw near to him. Speak Your comforting words to him through me, and help me to always be committed to helping him through his trouble and grief. May my love for him be like a soothing balm in the midst of his struggles. And may he know You more because of me. Amen.

Oops

For I am the least of the apostles and do not even
deserve to be called an apostle, because I persecuted
the church of God. But by the grace of God I am what
I am, and his grace to me was not without effect.

I CORINTHIANS 15:9-10

Father, I'm so glad You love me even when I blow it
and make mistakes, even when I am dead wrong and
off course. I confess I don't have it all together—and yet
You still use me in my teen's life. Amazing!

Lord, I need Your comfort. I know You still love me,
but I feel so bad about the way I've handled some situations in our family. Looking back, I can see that some of
the decisions I've made were not helpful. I know I'll never
be a perfect parent—far from it!—so I ask that You will
forgive me and help my teen to forgive me too. Help me
to be quick to repent, to learn from my mistakes, and to
always seek Your guidance. Remind me to take the log
out of my own eye before I try to take the speck out of
my teen's eye. Fill me with Your Spirit, and let the fruit
of the Spirit grow in me. Thank You for covering my
sin—and my mistakes. Your grace to me is not without
effect! Amen.

Sometimes I Want to Give Up

Let us not become weary in doing good, for at the
proper time we will reap a harvest if we do not give up.

GALATIANS 6:9

Lord, help me to never give up on my teen. Sometimes
I feel weary and worn out, and I wonder if she will
ever accept the things I've shared and lived out. I keep
sowing seed, but I don't know if any of it is taking root
in her heart. Where her heart is hard, Lord, soften it with
Your love. Where her heart is full of weeds, tenderly make
an opening for the planting of Your Word. And where
her heart is shallow, find the openings where Your Word
can go deep and thrive.

Open my eyes, Lord, so I can see some growth in
my teen's life. May the things You lead me to say and do
bear some fruit. God, give me hope! Help me trust that
You are at work in her and that I can look forward to an
abundant harvest. And in the meantime, help me continue to diligently care for my teen just as a conscientious
farmer tends his crop.

I ask all these things in Your name. Amen.

Can I Hear an Amen?

Like cold water to a weary soul
is good news from a distant land.

PROVERBS 25:25

Lord, I have poured my life into my teen's life. I have tried to teach and train him well. And most of the time, he has listened and applied to his life the things he is hearing and seeing. It's been pretty easy up to now, but as his world expands, he is hearing more and more bad information. His convictions are challenged every day, and that has to be causing some internal conflict.

So, God, would You bring other people into my teen's life who can shout a hefty *amen* to the things he has learned? Would You use others to confirm and validate the instruction we have given him? When he is wavering, lead him to supportive people who will assure him that the things he has learned from us and from You are true and dependable and beneficial. With so many negative messages coming at him from the media and from his friends, I pray You will surround him with positive relationships and role models.

And when our teen sees someone make a good decision, may he have the courage to encourage that person and say amen.

What Does My Teen Want?

And now these three remain: faith, hope and
love. But the greatest of these is love.

1 CORINTHIANS 13:13

Heavenly Father, day after day I bring my needs to
You. And day after day, my teenager looks to me
to take care of her needs. But she doesn't stop with her
needs; she also talks to me about the things she wants. And
she wants everything! (Am I like that with You, Lord?) I
confess that my first inclination is to give her as much as I
can. But You are teaching me that I could be causing her
to feel entitled to more and more. Help me to recognize
the difference between her needs and her wants and to
be smarter about saying yes and saying no.

I also pray that I would be able to give her the greatest
gift of all—love. Father, regardless of what I do or don't
give my daughter, I want her to know that she is worthy
to be loved and that I love her. Help me to give her more
of the love she so desperately needs and fewer of the
things she simply wants. May she discern the difference
and learn more and more about what true love—Your
love—looks like. Amen.

Giving Up Control

Train a child in the way he should go,
and when he is old he will not turn from it.

PROVERBS 22:6

Father, You are the perfect parent. You don't control everything in my life; You allow me to make my own decisions (and make plenty of mistakes) so I can learn and grow and become mature. God, help me to do the same for my teen. I confess that I tend to control too much and to worry when he is on his own. Help me trust You more!

I'm willing, Lord. Show me where I can step back and give my son more control of his life. Help me to talk less and to show more, walking beside him as he takes more and more steps on his own. As I give him bigger opportunities to be responsible, strengthen him to make good decisions and show himself to be dependable. When I'm tempted to give him a lecture, help us to have an open dialogue instead. When my first inclination is to tell him what to do, help me give him a chance to try a few things on his own and learn through experience. O Father, make me a better teacher, more like You, so my son can live well on his own and be salt and light in a dark and tasteless world. Amen.

Loss

And I will ask the Father, and he will give you
another Counselor to be with you forever.

JOHN 14:16

Lord, I hate the thought of my daughter experiencing loss, but I know that every kid gets hurt sometimes. Does she feel free to come talk to me about her pain, or is she embarrassed or afraid to let me know when something bad happens? I suppose she's been hurt more than I know, and she'll undoubtedly be hurt again. My heart aches when I think about that. O God, I pray that You would use every hurt she has experienced, every loss she will one day suffer, to draw her closer to me and to You. In her pain, may she find the support of true friends and learn the value of healthy relationships. In every struggle, I pray that You would make her heart better, not bitter.

Father, as my daughter experiences more freedom and responsibility and independence, help her depend less on me and more on You. Thank You for being such a wonderful Counselor to me. I know that You will be the same for her—forever. Amen.

Whom Is This About?

Do nothing out of selfish ambition or vain conceit, but
in humility consider others better than yourselves.
Each of you should look not only to your own
interests, but also to the interests of others.

PHILIPPIANS 2:3-4

Lord, I've noticed a troubling trend: I seem to be disciplining my child in anger rather than for his benefit. Why can't I remain calm when he chooses poorly? Am I depending on his performance to make me feel good as a parent, basing my self-esteem on his success? Search my heart, O God. Help me to know that I am valuable to You; pour Your love into my heart.

As I become securer in You, help me to show my son favor regardless of whether he is doing well. May I never lay the responsibility for my self-worth on his shoulders or expect him to meet my needs. Save me from selfishness, Lord, and help me to focus on what is best for him. When I discipline him, may I only be thinking of him, wanting what's best for him, acting for his good and not in anger. Empower me to look to his interests and not be so concerned about my own. I know that You will take care of me so I can take care of him. Thank You! Amen.

Secret Behavior

If any of you lacks wisdom, he should ask
God, who gives generously to all without
finding fault, and it will be given to him.

JAMES 1:5

Father, I don't know what my teen is doing, but I'm pretty sure it isn't good. And because I don't know what is going on, I don't know what to do. I look to You, Father—would You give me wisdom and insight and understanding so I will know what to do in my situation at home?

Speak to me through Your Word. Help me connect with caring people—my pastor, a counselor, family members, friends, whomever—and speak to me through them. Reveal any secrets that could be holding my teen captive. Give me sharp perception so I will notice the telltale signs that will lead me to the root of the problem. God, You know all things, and You see everything, including what's going on in my teen's heart. But I don't even know what's happening on the outside, let alone on the inside. Show me what I need to know to be an effective parent. Illumine my path. And when I do find out what's going on, touch my heart with compassion and my mind with understanding so I can communicate helpfully with my teen. Thank You, God, for caring. Amen.

Thankful in Every Situation

We rejoice in the hope of the glory of God. Not only so,
but we also rejoice in our sufferings, because we know
that suffering produces perseverance; perseverance,
character; and character, hope. And hope does not
disappoint us, because God has poured out his love into
our hearts by the Holy Spirit, whom he has given us.

ROMANS 5:2-5

Lord, how can I possibly rejoice in sufferings? I'm willing to believe that suffering produces perseverance and character and hope. Believing is one thing, but actually rejoicing in what I trust is true is another thing altogether. Father, I pray that my feelings will not overwhelm me in difficult times. Help me to be honest about what I'm feeling, to express and release my pent-up sorrow and hurt and joy in healthy ways, and to continue talking with You about my emotions. I know You created me not only to think and choose but to feel as well, and I want to learn everything my emotional responses can teach me.

And God, especially when I'm struggling, I pray that You would help me to sense Your presence, to trust that You are guiding me, and to remain focused on the good things You are doing. Lord, I have hope in You. Amen.

Don't Let Sin Reign

Do not let sin reign in your mortal body so that you obey its evil desires. Do not offer the parts of your body to sin, as instruments of wickedness, but rather offer yourselves to God, as those who have been brought from death to life; and offer the parts of your body to him as instruments of righteousness. For sin shall not be your master, because you are not under law, but under grace.

ROMANS 6:12-14

Lord, my teen is not doing so well, and the situation is tearing me apart. I feel as if I'm watching my beautiful child being swallowed up in a giant sinkhole of sin, and nothing I say seems to help. I try to have open, respectful conversations with her, but she is unresponsive to me. All the boundaries, rules, and consequences I have set in place have been about as effective as a small drizzling rain on a raging forest fire.

Father, would You get her attention and throw her a lifeline? May the pain of her foolish choices become greater than the pleasure she is getting from her inappropriate actions. Somehow, I pray that You would help her come to her senses, turn around, and start walking on a healthier and more productive path—a path of righteousness. I love You, Lord, and pray that You would help my daughter sense Your love this week. Amen.

Is This Supposed to Be Fun?

I do not understand what I do. For what I want
to do I do not do, but what I hate I do.

ROMANS 7:15

Heavenly Father, my teen tells me he doesn't want to
be doing the things he's doing, but he gets trapped
and ends up someplace he doesn't want to be. I ask for
two things, Father. First, would You show me why my
teen is struggling? Lead me as I develop a plan and make
changes in our home to keep my teen safe and help him
get back on track. Reveal the root of the problem and keep
us from slapping a Band-Aid on a serious situation.

Second, would You soften my teen's heart so we can
have good talks and so he can accept what I have to say?
Help me to listen to him, to assure him that I'm on his
side, and to build a relational bridge. Help him not to
become defensive, not to shut me out, and to see the pos-
sibility of a better way to live.

I ask these things in Your Son's name. Amen.

Hope's Anticipation

In this hope we were saved. But hope that is seen is no hope at all. Who hopes for what he already has? But if we hope for what we do not yet have, we wait for it patiently.

ROMANS 8:24-25

Father, my hope, my trust, my faith…it's all in You. Where would I be without You? I'd be in a heap of trouble, I'm sure. But I know that You will bring to completion the good work You have begun in my family. I don't see how You will do it, and I don't know when, but I do know You. So my prayer is that You would help me trust You more and wait more patiently as You intervene in my teen's life. Father, protect her from the harmful influences all around her. Keep her safe, and let Your peace guard her heart and mind. May she be able to defend herself against those who do not have her best interest in mind.

And when I begin to give up hope, when I'm tempted to despair, interrupt my thoughts, O God, with a verse, a song, a word from a friend…anything that can remind me that I always have hope in You. Amen.

It's Going to Work Out

We know that in all things God works for
the good of those who love him,
who have been called according to his purpose.

ROMANS 8:28

Lord, You have always been faithful to me in the past, so I know that I'll get through my teen's adolescence. I am completely confident that You have a wonderful future for our family. I know that You will someday turn our ashes into beauty, our mourning into dancing, and our sadness into joy.

But trusting You for the future seems to be easier than trusting You for today. The future is so "out there," and today is here and now. I pray that You would calm my anxious thoughts and help me trust You for good things today. Sustain me, encourage me, and touch my heart with an awareness of Your love. Help me to find joy in each day—each moment!—so I don't look back someday and realize I took this season for granted. I trust in You, Lord. Amen.

Inclusive Love

I am convinced that neither death nor life, neither angels
nor demons, neither the present nor the future, nor
any powers, neither height nor depth, nor anything
else in all creation, will be able to separate us from
the love of God that is in Christ Jesus our Lord.

ROMANS 8:38-39

Lord, You love me all the time—not only when I do
well but also when I make choices and decisions that
don't follow Your desires. Thank You for a love that can
weather all storms and that isn't diminished by a cloudy
day. You are a friend for all times and will never allow
anything to come between me and Your love.

Father, make me more like You! Help me to love
my teen the way You love me. Let Your love flow freely
through me to him and never stop. Show me how to love
him with my words, my actions, and my decisions. May
he know that nothing can separate him from my love for
him because it is from You. And keep me from spouting
out empty words and empty prayers. Please transform my
heart and my relationship with my son. Amen.

Encourage, Not Discourage

Fathers, do not embitter your children, or
they will become discouraged.

COLOSSIANS 3:21

Lord, You know (better than I do) my desires for my teen, my true motivation, and my feelings as I watch her mature. Please help me not to get carried away by my fears and concerns, always correcting and never encouraging. Fill me with Your Spirit so I will have love, peace, patience, gentleness, and self-control when I do need to correct her. Help me to build a relational bridge and to always move toward her—when she is walking uprightly and when she is stumbling. Nudge me when I need to remain silent, and push me when I need to speak up.

I want to stand in front of her less and walk beside her more, to always encourage and never discourage, to strengthen and empower her and build her up. Dear God, make me a refuge my daughter runs to in times of trouble, and save me from ever becoming a threatening or condemning influence in her life. I ask all these things in Your Son's name. Amen.

Weary and Weak

The LORD is the everlasting God,
the Creator of the ends of the earth.
He will not grow tired or weary,
and his understanding no one can fathom.
He gives strength to the weary
and increases the power of the weak.

ISAIAH 40:28-29

Lord, I praise You as the Creator of all and the ever-lasting God, the one who never grows weary. You never get tired...but loving my teen is wearing me out. I feel so weak; would You increase my strength? Empower me to do what I need to do and be who I need to be for my teen.

O God, I know his life isn't always easy either. Open my eyes so I will notice when he is weary. Help me understand what he needs and what is holding him back. Help me to be there for him when he is weak. As You strengthen me in my weariness, help me to be a strengthening influence in his life. As you empower me in my weakness, help me to impart Your power to him as well. I look to You, the everlasting God. Amen.

Renew Your Strength

Even youths grow tired and weary,
and young men stumble and fall;
but those who hope in the LORD
will renew their strength.
They will soar on wings like eagles;
they will run and not grow weary,
they will walk and not be faint.

ISAIAH 40:30-31

Lord, I'll be the first to admit that I haven't done everything right with my kids, and I've often stumbled and occasionally fallen while trying to raise my family in a loving atmosphere. Our family has soared at times and floundered at others. We have run toward each other, and we have run away from each other. We've been inconsistent, but our bottom line is this: We want to walk in a manner worthy of You.

I'm so thankful that You've always invited me to bring my shortcomings to You and put my hope in You. You've been so patient with me, so willing to pick me up when I plummet and to energize me when I feel as if I've gone as far as I can go. Whether my family is flying, running, walking, or even stumbling, my hope will always be in You. Thank You, Lord. Amen.

A New Low

I sink in the miry depths, where there is no foothold.
I have come into the deep waters; the floods engulf me.
I am worn out calling for help; my throat is parched.
My eyes fail, looking for my God.

PSALM 69:2-3

Lord, I see many families around me struggling and loads of kids acting with disobedience and disrespect. The youth culture has stooped to a new low, and my friends with teenage kids feel lost and don't know what to do. They appear to be sinking in miry situations we never saw coming.

Lord, hear their pleas and reveal Yourself to them. Use me and my family as a lifeline of hope and a firm place to stand so our friends won't be engulfed by the flood of evil in our world. Help us provide a place of rest for them. Use us to affirm the truth and strengthen families who are fighting against lies. Give us spiritual perception so we can help them see You working in the midst of their struggles. God, our hope is in You, and we trust that You will save us! Amen.

When I Need a Break

My heart is in anguish within me;
the terrors of death assail me.
Fear and trembling have beset me;
horror has overwhelmed me.
I said, "Oh, that I had the wings of a dove!
I would fly away and be at rest."

PSALM 55:4-6

Father, I feel as though I'm at the end of my rope, worn out, spent, overwhelmed. With so much pressure—from raising teens, being a spouse, coordinating schedules, dealing with health issues, feeling unappreciated and undervalued—I'm tempted to run away to find some rest. I know I can't do that, but that's how I feel.

Lord, would You calm and soothe my aching heart and keep my emotions from running wild? When the raging current of my feelings carries me away from You, would You reach out and catch me, pull me close, and let me hear Your voice? I love You, and I know that You are the only one who can save me. I also love my family, and I want You to love them through me. Thank You for not condemning me when I experience these episodes of doubt. I look forward to watching You calm the storm. In the meantime, will You calm my heart? Thank You. Amen.

The Big Picture

Since, then, you have been raised with Christ, set
your hearts on things above, where Christ is seated
at the right hand of God. Set your minds on things
above, not on earthly things. For you died, and
your life is now hidden with Christ in God.

COLOSSIANS 3:1-3

Lord, I need Your help knowing what is important and what isn't. I don't have the time or energy to focus on everything, so would You help me know what to set my heart and mind on and what to simply let go? I pray for insight so I will know what things will have a long-term effect and what will simply fade away. I live in such a day-to-day world, I tend to focus on little details and forget about the big picture. Help me look at our family's needs from Your perspective. Open my eyes so I can assess our family's situation in the light of what's really important.

God, help me set my heart and my mind on things above, on the invisible things, and not on the first thing I see. Thank You for sharing Your perspective with me and for giving me the wisdom and insight I need to guide my family. I'm so grateful that You have hidden my life in You! Amen!

Who, Me? Offend Someone?

Search me, O God, and know my heart;
test me and know my anxious thoughts.
See if there is any offensive way in me,
and lead me in the way everlasting.

PSALM 139:23-24

Heavenly Father, I couldn't say it any better than David did. I probably don't have a clue how often I offend or hurt people. I imagine my casual remarks sometimes make people feel terrible. And worse yet, those remarks surely reveal what's actually in my heart. O God, search me, know me, test me, and lead me to a better place.

I tell myself I don't expect my teen to be perfect, but I have a hunch that my words and actions communicate something different. Do I offend and hurt her? Do I push her away? I don't want to do that to her or to be that kind of person. Show me how I lay unrealistic expectations on her, how I celebrate her victories halfheartedly, how I affirm my love for her when she succeeds more than I do when she fails. I repent, Lord. Cleanse my heart, and help me make the changes I need to make. You always think the best of me. Help me think the best of everyone in my family. Amen.

Waiting on Your Word

When our words came, I ate them;
they were my joy and my heart's delight,
for I bear your name,
O LORD God Almighty.

JEREMIAH 15:16

Lord, just when I need You most, You speak to me. I love to hear Your voice in Your Word, in my thoughts, and in conversations with people who don't even know You are encouraging me through them. Thank You for speaking to me, for giving me wisdom and insight that penetrates to my very soul, brings life to me, strengthens my heart, and brings me joy. I am amazed that You not only care about me, You actually talk with me! How can I thank You enough!

Dear God, I want to lead my family to You. Help me to bear Your name—to represent You to each member of my family and to bring each one to You in prayer. Continue to make me more like You so I can be an effective ambassador of Your love to my family. What a privilege to carry Your name! Help me to live a life that's worthy of this high calling. Amen.

When Your Teen Is
Spinning out of Control

I pray also that the eyes of your heart may be
enlightened in order that you may know the
hope to which he has called you, the riches of
his glorious inheritance in the saints, and his
incomparably great power for us who believe.

EPHESIANS 1:18-19

Lord, I have some very difficult decisions to make, and I want to choose well. I want to please You, to represent You well, and to do what's best for my teenager. Open the eyes of my heart so I will know what's really going on in his life and so I will focus on Your incomparably great power. Help me not to be distracted by the other responsibilities that I must attend to, and guide me in the direction that is most helpful for my son.

Lord, this is a stressful time for me. I pray that You would help me be the parent You have called me to be, to stand not only when everything is easy but also when difficulties arise. Help me to think clearly and not be overcome by adrenalin or runaway emotions. Give me Your wisdom so I don't react impulsively. And Lord, I pray that You would calm his heart and help him come to his senses. I pray in Your Son's name. Amen.

Protect My Teen

The Lord is faithful, and he will strengthen and
protect you from the evil one. We have confidence
in the Lord that you are doing and will continue to
do the things we command. May the Lord direct your
hearts into God's love and Christ's perseverance.

2 THESSALONIANS 3:3-5

Lord, thank You for being faithful to my teen and for
giving her strength. She lives in a difficult world and
constantly faces temptations and trials that could trip
her up. O Lord, please protect her. Deliver her from the
evil one, and direct her heart into Your love. Help her to
follow the good teaching she has received from me and
from other spiritual leaders. May she persevere by the
power of Your Spirit.

Father, please use my daughter as Your instrument of
peace in her friends' lives. May she lead others to You by
her example, and may she inspire others to persevere. I
have confidence in You that she will continue to grow and
mature and bear wonderful fruit. Thank You! Amen.

Laughter

He will yet fill your mouth with laughter
and your lips with shouts of joy.

JOB 8:21

Father, I'm realizing that I need to give my family more opportunities to have fun together. Laughter is so therapeutic—I pray that You'd give us a big dose of it! Show me how to enjoy the lighter side of life and not be so serious all the time. Help me to lighten up, to see the humor in everyday situations, and to smile and laugh more often. Remind me to not be so critical, dogmatic, judgmental, and negative.

Jesus, some of the stories You told were funny, and little children enjoyed being around You. I want to be more like You—a fun person to be with, a conduit of joy, and a channel of life. Help me delight in the good things You have done and are doing, and help me point them out to others. May the joy of my salvation bubble over onto my entire family. Soften our grumpy hearts and make us glad, relax our stern expressions and help us smile, and help us replace our biting words with blessings! Amen.

A Way of Escape

He will also provide a way out.

I CORINTHIANS 10:13

Lord, I spend too much time telling my teens what *not* to do and rarely offer better alternatives or healthier options. I have warned them about some of life's dangers, but I haven't always been compassionate when they get themselves into messy situations, and I've rarely equipped them in advance by showing them a way of escape. Lord, help me become a better teacher. Give me practical ideas to share with them that will empower them to avoid trouble when they see it coming their way. Fill my mouth with Your words so they will know that I love them and that I'm on their side as we face a common enemy.

And Lord, when my kids do fall into a hole, may the things I've taught them be like a ladder that helps them get out of the pit. When they find themselves in dark places, may Your Word and my words be like lights that lead them into the brightness of day. Thank You, God, that they never need to face a dead end because You will always provide a way out. Amen.

Sharing My Strength

Think how you have instructed many,
how you have strengthened feeble hands.
Your words have supported those who stumbled;
you have strengthened faltering knees.

JOB 4:3-4

Lord, do I instruct my teen effectively so he will thrive as he becomes more independent? Do I strengthen him so he can do Your work in his world? Do I support him when he stumbles? I want to do those things, but I confess that I haven't been as intentional about them as he needs me to be. And sometimes when I do try to strengthen him, it comes out all wrong. Lord, cleanse me, fill me, and help me to connect with my son and offer him the support he needs.

When he does stumble, help me move toward him, not away from him. Even when he offends me and violates all that I stand for, fill my heart with compassion. When he falls, show me how to help him up. When he makes mistakes, give me encouraging words to share. When he is embarrassed by his failings, may he know that I am never embarrassed of him. And when he makes terrible choices and tries to hide from me, help me to move toward him and assure him that I love him—for that's the way You have treated me. Thank You.

A Special Purpose

The LORD will fulfill his purpose for me;
your love, O LORD, endures forever—
do not abandon the works of your hands.

PSALM 138:8

Lord, You have created each one of us in this world for a purpose, and today I pray that You would help my teen find hers. I'm thankful that You will never abandon her; may she never abandon You or Your plan for her life. I know You will fulfill Your purpose for her; may she cooperate with You and allow You to work in her life.

Father, You have given my daughter so much potential and so many gifts. Help her know how to use those gifts. Draw her close to You as You guide her toward a wonderful future. Fill her with love, patience, and tenacity so she will keep moving with You toward Your purpose for her life. And show me how I can help her follow You into her full potential. Amen.

Offering Encouragement Purposefully

My purpose is that they may be encouraged in heart and united in love, so that they may have the full riches of complete understanding, in order that they may know the mystery of God, namely, Christ, in whom are hidden all the treasures of wisdom and knowledge.

COLOSSIANS 2:2-3

Father, in this season of my life, may I be purposeful about encouraging my teen's heart. Help me to connect with him even as I'm giving him more freedom and helping him to stand on his own. May my words and my actions empower him to know You better. May he follow my example, engage "the mystery of God," and be drawn to Your treasures of wisdom and knowledge.

And Lord, when struggles come, may he cling tighter and tighter to You. May he never give up or abandon You, Father, and may our hearts always be united in love. Amen.

My Wounded Teen

My friends and companions avoid
me because of my wounds;
my neighbors stay far away.

PSALM 38:11

Lord, I feel so bad for my teen. He's having a hard time finding a place to fit in at school. All the social circles seem to exclude him, so he feels as if he doesn't have any friends and doesn't know how to find any. He doesn't want to go to school because he gets rejected, ridiculed, and bullied. He doesn't even want to go to church anymore. He compounds his isolation by rushing home and escaping with video games and the computer. I fear for his heart and feel his wounding.

Father, would You fill his empty places and bring into his life a good friend who can walk with him during this time? Lead him to positive conversations and interactions at school so he can see that he really does have something to contribute. And help me to be sensitive to his needs and encouraging in my words so he always knows that he is loved and accepted at home.

I hurt as my teen hurts, so I ask that You would comfort us both. Amen.

Rejected by Friends

All my intimate friends detest me;
those I love have turned against me.

JOB 19:19

Lord, my daughter is struggling in school—not with classes, but with friends. For years, we've valued her and honored her as a princess, but this year the kids at school have snubbed her and left her feeling devalued and lonely. She sits by herself during lunch and walks alone between classes. No one asks her to come over and hang out after school. Her rejection brings me to tears. If I could give up all my friends so she could have just one, I'd do it.

How I pray that just one other girl would come alongside her so she would not have to be so alone. Dear God, may someone notice her, smile at her, say hi…anything that would give her hope of finding a friend. Bring a safe person into her life, and protect her from reaching out in desperation to people who would lead her astray. And in the meantime, assure her that to us, she is still a princess. Amen.

Clean Hands

Who may ascend the hill of the Lord?
Who may stand in his holy place?
He who has clean hands and a pure heart,
who does not lift up his soul to an
idol or swear by what is false.
He will receive blessing from the Lord
and vindication from God his Savior.

PSALM 24:3-5

Lord, I want to have clean hands and a pure heart. I want to live a life of integrity—for Your glory, for my good, and for the sake of my family and others who watch my life. Help me to be an example to my teens, showing them how to stand for what is true, how to make the right decision even when it's difficult, how to remain loyal to friends, how to honor You, and how to be a blessing to people who are suffering adversity.

Lord, may I spend more time showing my kids how to live and less time talking about how *not* to live. In a simple, quiet way, may I inspire my kids to follow You. In Your holy name I ask these things. Amen.

Blessed Is the Man

Blessed is the man
who makes the LORD his trust,
who does not look to the proud,
to those who turn aside to false gods.

PSALM 40:4

Lord, You are my trust. In good times and difficult times, I have looked to You and not to the proud—people who trust in the false gods of our technologically advanced and materialistic society.

Lord, I want my teen to know that he too can make You his trust and be confident that You'll show up at just the right time and honor Your commitment to him. Assure him that he can count on You when he can't count on others, and he can trust You when no one else does. Bless him as You have blessed me, and may he see me as an example of Your blessing—an example that he wants to follow. Amen.

Forgiveness

Therefore, as God's chosen people, holy and dearly loved, clothe yourselves with compassion, kindness, humility, gentleness and patience. Bear with each other and forgive whatever grievances you may have against one another. Forgive as the Lord forgave you.

COLOSSIANS 3:12-13

Lord, I want my teen to know how to forgive, how to be compassionate and kind, how to be gentle and patient, and how to live in relationship with others. I pray that she would prioritize her relationships so highly that she would be willing to forgive people who have wronged her and to apologize and ask for forgiveness when she offends someone else.

And I pray that You would use me as an example in her life. Lord, have I been holding on to a grudge instead of forgiving someone? Have I offended someone, and do I need to apologize and ask for forgiveness? God, I see in Your Word that You value relationships. Help me to follow Your example so my daughter can follow mine. Amen.

A Place of Rest

Come to me, all you who are weary and burdened,
and I will give you rest. Take my yoke upon You
and learn from me, for I am gentle and humble
in heart, and You will find rest for Your souls.
For my yoke is easy and my burden is light.

MATTHEW 11:28-30

Father, sometimes all I seem to be doing is correct-ing, disciplining, pointing out mistakes, and nagging about what my teens need to do. I want great things for them, but am I pushing too hard? Our home feels tense and rigid rather than restful and relaxing.

Lord, please help me create a relational atmosphere so my kids feel safe and free to let down their guard and be refreshed. Help me to be gentle with them. Humble my heart so I can care for them and not always be so concerned about myself. And help me provide a setting where my teens can unwind and find rest for their souls so that they might get a taste of who You are. Help me make life easier for them, not harder, and may my expec-tations be light, not heavy. Amen.

Hope in a Difficult Time

There is surely a future hope for you,
and your hope will not be cut off.

PROVERBS 23:18

Father, I pray that You would touch my heart. I need assurance that You are involved in my life not only on sunny days but also when dark clouds of doubt and despair roll in. I confess that when my teen is struggling, I struggle too. I'm so concerned for him...I see the mess he's in, and I tend to focus on his problems instead of Your incomprehensible love for us.

O God, would You help me sense Your presence in our home so that I might have hope? Help me to believe that regardless of what the circumstances seem to say, You know everything that is going on, and You can touch my son right where he is. I pray that You would use this situation somehow to help him to know You better. Father, thank You for Your commitment to never leave us or forsake us—even in situations like ours. We trust You to lead and guide us as we sort this out. In Your Son's name we pray. Amen.

Mourning Loss

Jesus wept.

JOHN 11:35

Heavenly Father, my teen has just experienced a difficult loss, and her pain is nearly overwhelming her. I can't take away the pain, so help me to simply be with her, to comfort her, and to provide a safe place for her to feel what she's feeling. O God, please save her from burying her feelings. Help her express and release her sorrow in tears, in conversations with me, in heartfelt prayers to You, and in other constructive ways. Draw her and me together as we process this difficult situation together.

Would You go beyond what I can do and comfort her in Your own special way? I pray that this loss would drive her to You for comfort, and that in You, she would find relief and hope. I pray that this loss would cause her to reflect on her life, it's purpose, her priorities, and her need for You. May her tears bring her closer to You and to me. Amen.

Bitterness

Do not let any unwholesome talk come out of your
mouths, but only what is helpful for building others
up according to their needs, that it may benefit those
who listen...Get rid of all bitterness, rage and anger,
brawling and slander, along with every form of malice.
Be kind and compassionate to one another, forgiving
each other, just as in Christ God forgave You.

EPHESIANS 4:29-32

Lord, my teen is suffering from more cruelty, rejection, hurtful words, bullying, and criticism than ever before. I pray that instead of becoming bitter, he will sense Your compassion and understanding and will grow into a better relationship with You. I pray that he will draw closer to me as well as I comfort him, listen to him, and help him express his feeling constructively.

May the things I have taught him about forgiveness and trusting You come to his mind and help him understand the value of walking blamelessly. Protect my son, dear God, so he won't be crippled by bitterness. Help him to learn from this situation and rise above it. Thank You. Amen.

Jesus Saves—I Don't

Here is a trustworthy saying that deserves full acceptance: Christ Jesus came into the world to save sinners—of whom I am the worst.

TIMOTHY 1:15

Lord, my new teen thinks that I'm her hero, that I can do no wrong, and that I will be with her forever. You and I know that this is far from the truth! Help me gently guide her away from depending on me so she can depend more on You.

She doesn't seem to notice or remember all the times I've failed her. But I know that someday, she'll have to take me down off this pedestal. When that day comes and she faces the fact that I'm not perfect, give her assurance that we're all still here, we all still love each other, and You will provide everything we need. Amen.

Making Good Choices

My son, if sinners entice you,
do not give in to them.

PROVERBS 1:10

Lord, I've done my best to teach my teen how to make good choices and to stand up for what is right in this world. Now I entrust him to You and pray that all the lessons he has learned will ring loud and clear in his ears when he is enticed by the snares of sin. I pray that Your Holy Spirit would nudge his heart every time he is tempted by the allure of evil. Strengthen him to stand firm against the forces of darkness that would try to tear down his faith. Support him with Your presence, Your Word, and faithful friends and mentors who can encourage him and build up his faith.

And if he ever falters, Lord, assure him that You are never out of reach and will never walk away from him. Help him to accept the fact that he is not perfect, to rejoice because You will always love him, and to look for others whom he can encourage along the way. Amen.

Enjoying the Years

Dear friend, I pray that you may enjoy good
health and that all may go well with you,
even as your soul is getting along well.

3 JOHN 2

Lord, I don't want to be so busy and intent on work that I ignore my family's needs. Nudge me when I am selfishly spending too much time at work and promoting myself and my own agenda. Guide my thoughts as I reevaluate my priorities. Show me creative ways to have fun with my family and show them how much I love them.

I ask for wisdom so I can find a helpful balance between my work life and my family life. Help me pay attention to my body and do what is necessary to keep healthy so I will be around to enjoy my kids' kids. Help me organize my life in such a way that I may enjoy each day and each person in my family. Thank You for the life and the family You've given me! Amen.

Being Content

I have learned to be content whatever the circumstances.
I know what it is to be in need, and I know what it
is to have plenty. I have learned the secret of being
content in any and every situation, whether well
fed or hungry, whether living in plenty or in want.

PHILIPPIANS 4:11-12

Father, I am often repulsed by my culture's neurotic compulsion to have more, make more, and be more. (But when I'm not repulsed by it, I'm tempted to go with the flow! Forgive me.) I hate to see parents' career ambitions take priority and their families lose out.

I don't want to be that kind of parent. I would hate to have everything but lose what is most important. Lord, please help me remember what is at stake if I start to ignore my family. Save me from ever becoming so involved in business and other interests that I ignore the people I love the most. Father, help me be content with my possessions and my standard of living, to enjoy those things appropriately, and to always be thankful for them. May the relationships in my family always take priority over my workplace relationships. Help me to show the people in my own home how much I love and value them. Amen.

A New Creation

Therefore, if anyone is in Christ, he is a new creation;
the old has gone, the new has come!

2 CORINTHIANS 5:17

Lord, is the old really gone? Have I allowed the past to stay in the past, or is it still affecting my present in negative ways? I pray that You would show me if I am stuck because I haven't yet appropriately responded to important experiences in my past. Illumine my heart so I can make any necessary adjustments and move on. I trust that even though I will never have a better past, I can deal with it and not let it control my present or hurt my family.

I rejoice with You, Lord—I *am* a new creation! Guide my steps in this new way of living. And likewise, guide my daughter so she can grow freely and unencumbered by chains from her past. Deliver her, God, from bondage to any negative experiences she's had in her short life. I ask for wisdom and grace so I can help her respond appropriately to her past, encourage her to move on, and relate to her as a new creation. Amen.

Guard Your Heart

Above all else, guard your heart, for
it is the wellspring of life.

PROVERBS 4:23

Father, in a world of rampant seduction, lust, and self-ishness, I pray that You would guard my teen's heart. Speak to him through me and other adults, through songs and sermons, through Your Word, and through Your Spirit's gentle whispers in his heart. I pray that You will surround him with friends who will mitigate the world's harmful effects. Give him wisdom to distinguish between the influences and activities that will strengthen his heart and the ones that will hurt him.

Father, I know that my son's heart will be hurt from time to time. When that happens, please apply Your healing touch. May his heart be full of love and joy and life, and may it always beat for You. Amen.

Finding the Lost

I tell you the truth, [the shepherd] is happier about that one sheep [that he recovered] than about the ninety-nine that did not wander off. In the same way your Father in heaven is not willing that any of these little ones should be lost.

MATTHEW 18:13-15

Father, I know how much You care about the lost. And I know we should search for the lost and help them find their way. But I always thought I could tell who was lost and who wasn't. I never realized that a lost one was sleeping down the hallway from me every night. I'm sorry, Lord, for being so overconfident in my ability to see deeply into people's hearts. Help me to stop making rash judgments about people and squeezing them into neat little boxes.

O God, use my life as an example for others. May I be a road map that helps the people around me stay on course. And should any of them ever get lost, give me grace and wisdom to point them in the right direction. May I never ignore the lost—especially when they live in my own home. Amen.

There's a Greater Plan

O LORD, what is man that you care for him,
the son of man that you think of him?
Man is like a breath;
his days are like a fleeting shadow.

PSALM 144:3-4

Lord, I need a new perspective on time. My lifetime is so short in the light of history and eternity. And this time of my teen's adolescence is even shorter—just eight years, or one-tenth of her life. Help me to make wise investments of time and energy into her life now, while I have this unique opportunity to gently guide her through this transitional stage. Give me the wisdom to continually prioritize our relationship. Open my mind to creative ways to encourage her, have fun with her, and let her know I love her.

Someday soon, Father, she will step out of our home and into a new stage of her life. I pray that when that day comes, I will be able to look back on these years and feel good about our life together. Amen.

The Refuge

The LORD is a refuge for the oppressed,
a stronghold in times of trouble.
Those who know your name will trust in you,
for you, LORD, have never forsaken those who seek you.

PSALM 9:9-10

Lord, when my teen hurts, I hurt. When things aren't going well for him, they usually aren't going well for me either. When my son gets rejected, I feel rejected. When he doesn't get picked to be on a team or in a circle of friends, I feel forsaken. May my son always know he can safely share his feelings with me. And when he does...

...help me lead him back to You. Make me compassionate and empathetic in his times of sorrow, and then show me how I can direct his attention to You. Use my example and my words to teach him how to run to You, to make You his refuge and stronghold, and to know Your name and trust in You. Thank You for never forsaking or ignoring him—especially when he's hurting. Amen.

Holding on to Hope

May the God of hope fill you with all joy and peace
as you trust in him, so that you may overflow
with hope by the power of the Holy Spirit.

ROMANS 15:13

Lord, I'm holding on to hope as my daughter and I wrestle through her adolescent years. I feel as if the little girl who went to bed last night woke up this morning as a completely different person. This season is challenging for everyone in my family, and we've discovered that we need to spend a little more time talking about some important issues.

Fill me with joy and peace, O God. May I overflow with hope by the power of Your Spirit, and may that hope touch everyone in my home as well. The difficulties we are facing now loom large in our eyes, but all things are possible with You. This is not the end of the story, so for now, I'm holding on to hope as I hold on to You. Thank You for never letting go of us. Amen.

What More Could I Ask For?

For this reason, since the day we heard about you,
we have not stopped praying for you and asking God
to fill you with the knowledge of his will through all
spiritual wisdom and understanding. And we pray this
in order that you may live a life worthy of the Lord
and may please him in every way: bearing fruit in every
good work, growing in the knowledge of God, being
strengthened with all power according to his glorious
might so that you may have great endurance and
patience, and joyfully giving thanks to the Father.

COLOSSIANS 1:9-12

Father, just as Paul never stopped praying for the people he was teaching, may I never stop praying for my family and especially for my teen. Fill all of us with the knowledge of Your will, and give me the spiritual wisdom and understanding I need to build a strong relationship with my son and walk alongside him during his teen years. Strengthen me, dear Lord, so I will have power to patiently endure this season of ups and downs, advances and setbacks.

God, Paul called Your might *glorious*. Help me to have confidence in You, to see how glorious Your might is, and to joyfully give thanks to You in expectation of all You will do in my family. Amen.

Hang In There

But now trouble comes to you, and you are discouraged;
it strikes you, and you are dismayed.
Should not your piety be your confidence
and your blameless ways your hope?
Consider now: Who, being innocent, has ever perished?
Where were the upright ever destroyed?

JOB 4:5-7

Lord, help me not to be discouraged because of the trouble surrounding my teen. You have not abandoned us in all our issues and conflict, so I need not be dismayed. I pray that You would use this situation to strengthen the relationships in my family and help every person in my household depend on You.

Father, I'm anything but blameless, and if I had to put my confidence in my piety, I'd be in trouble. Most of the time, I wouldn't describe myself as innocent or upright. But You are the holy one, and my confidence and hope are in You. Thank You! Amen.

Living in Freedom

It is for freedom that Christ has set us free.
Stand firm, then, and do not let yourselves
be burdened again by a yoke of slavery.

GALATIANS 5:1

Heavenly Father, You have set me free—thank You! Lead me, Lord, as I move my family away from a slavish adherence to rules. Show us how to root out legalism and enjoy authentic relationships. Speak through me so my family always hears words of love, acceptance, and forgiveness instead of condemnation. When I have to correct and discipline my teens, empower me to do it in a way that affirms my commitment to help them flourish. Teach us to live as free people!

I receive Your word to me today. I want to stand firm. God, please sound the alert in my heart whenever my family starts living like slaves again. Give me wisdom to discern when we are slipping back into our old habits. Thank You for removing our yoke of slavery and inviting us to walk with You. Amen.

Hard Work

Whatever you do, work at it with all your heart, as
working for the Lord, not for men, since you know
that you will receive an inheritance from the Lord
as a reward. It is the Lord Christ you are serving.

COLOSSIANS 3:23-24

Lord, I want to pour my life into my teens. Help me
not to take a vacation from teaching them Your principles and sharing Your wisdom with them. Fill me with
Your Spirit every day so I will have the patience, endurance, and strength to persevere and not give up. Give
me wisdom so I will be an effective parent and not waste
energy spinning my wheels. When I begin to lose hope,
remind me of small victories that will inspire me to continue working hard.

And if my kids ever quit accepting my input, I pray
that You would help me learn new ways of communicating the truth to them. Regardless of whether they're
doing well, may I never quit working at loving them
better. Amen.

Have Some Fun

So I commend the enjoyment of life, because nothing
is better for a man under the sun than to eat and drink
and be glad. Then joy will accompany him in his work all
the days of the life God has given him under the sun.

ECCLESIASTES 8:15

Father, I confess that I am often an either-or kind of
person. Focusing on one thing at a time is easy for
me. I pray You would help me to be more of a both-and
person and to know how to work toward two seemingly
contradictory objectives at the same time.

Lord, show me ways to make our family life fun even
while I am teaching my teens to be responsible. Guide us
into a balanced lifestyle that encourages trustworthiness
while celebrating life with joy. Help me laugh more, tell
more jokes, find the humor in life, and share some fun (if
somewhat embarrassing) stories from my past. May my
teens enjoy being around me, and may I provide them with
an example of a life lived with abundant joy. Amen.

Above All, Love

I pray that you, being rooted and established in love, may
have power, together with all the saints, to grasp how
wide and long and high and deep is the love of Christ, and
to know this love that surpasses knowledge—that you
may be filled to the measure of all the fullness of God.

EPHESIANS 3:17-19

Gracious heavenly Father, You have loved me in ways
I never could have dreamed of. You have been with
me in good times and stood by me in difficult times.
You've loved me in the sunshine and in the rain. Thank
You for walking with me, for pouring Your life into me,
and for speaking gentle words of wisdom when I need
them the most. Thank You for always providing what I
need and not always giving me what I want.

Help me love my children as You have loved me—
when they are little and when they are adults, when they
are soaring and when they appear to be sinking. At all
times, in all circumstances, may Your love for me overflow onto them, and may my love for them point them
to You. Amen.

I Will Never Leave You

Keep your lives free from the love of money and
be content with what you have, because God has
said, "Never will I leave you; never will I forsake you."

HEBREWS 13:5

Father, I have so many reasons to thank You and to
celebrate Your goodness. I confess that I often grumble
and complain, but now I choose to repent. Help me to be
content with the fabulous blessings You have given me,
especially Your amazing promise to never leave me.

Father, when my kids are struggling, I pray that You
would touch their hearts and remind them of the reasons they can be thankful. May contentment characterize their lives. When their difficulties begin to pull me
down, open my eyes to see past the circumstances and
focus on their tender hearts, the wonderful gifts You have
put in their lives, and Your promise of a bright future for
them. Amen.

Other Great Harvest House
Books by Mark Gregston...

Parenting Today's Teens

Mark pours his experience with kids in crisis into a daily devotional. These short readings are filled with Scripture and real-life examples of young people who have successfully emerged from serious struggles.

When Your Teen Is Struggling

Is your teen exhibiting destructive or unhealthy behaviors and actions? Mark offers biblical guidance, encouraging stories, and a fresh message of hope as he shares the keys to turn parenting struggles into success.

What's Happening to My Teen?

Mark offers wise counsel that will help you succeed at one of the most difficult tasks you've ever encountered. This book provides the scriptural insight and the skills you need to see your family thrive during your children's challenging teen years.